Conclusion

About the Author

Resources

Writing and dissecting an agent acquisition letter and other resources.

<u>Simple Writing Strategies Presents:</u>

Super Simple Strategies To Write Any Book For Profit in 30 days or less.

Even If You've Never Written A Lick Of Content In Your Life…

By Glen L K Palmer

Table of Contents

Disclaimer

Legal Notice:

While all attempts have been made to verify information provided in this publication, neither the Author nor the Publisher assumes any responsibility for errors, omissions, or contrary interpretation of the subject matter herein.

This publication is not intended for use as a source of legal, business, financial or accounting advice, and is to be used for informational purposes only.

The Publisher wants to stress that the information contained herein may be subject to varying state and/or local laws or regulations. All users are advised to retain competent counsel to determine what state and/or local laws or regulations may apply to the user's particular business.

The Purchaser or Reader of this publication assumes responsibility for the use of these materials and information. Adherence to all applicable laws and regulations, federal, state, and local, governing professional licensing, business practices, advertising, and all other aspects of doing business in the United States, United Kingdom, or any other jurisdiction is the sole responsibility of the Purchaser or Reader.

The Author and Publisher assume no responsibility or liability whatsoever on the behalf of any Purchaser or Reader of these materials.

Any perceived slights of specific people or organizations are unintentional.

Introduction

Hi there, first and foremost I want to thank you for purchasing Simple Writing Strategies – Super Simple Strategies To Write Any Book For Profit In 30 Days Or Less and putting your faith in me. I personally think you've made the right choice in choosing my book over all the others that are out there, as I will soon prove to you.

Now I know that you don't know me, but over the next few chapters and weeks I feel we're going to be good friends. In just a few short pages, you're going to learn super simple strategies and techniques, which will enable you to write a book on *any* subject in 30 days or less, even if you've never written a lick of content in your life. Exciting times indeed.

It's said that there is a book in everyone. Everyone has a story to tell, however, there is a popular belief that you need to be educated in creative writing to express your thoughts onto paper. I personally believe that this isn't true, and I'm living proof of this.

I've always been interested in storytelling, I can clearly remember the times, as a kid, when I sat around campfires telling my friends stories. I had a very active imagination, so I decided to give writing a try as a profession.

However, much like where you are right now, I had no idea on how to write a book. I didn't know where to start, what to write about, whether I should write fiction or non-fiction and don't get me started on grammar, spelling and punctuation.

Does this sound familiar?

So before I actually wrote my first book, I did a few years of intense work on studying various writing techniques and many other strategies.

I guess you may be wondering why I decided to write this book? Well, I can remember the years of me scouring the Internet, attending writing workshops and classes. It was a lot of hard work and I realised there wasn't anyone teaching what I discovered. Yes, there was a strategy being taught here, and a technique there, but I wanted to combine them all to make it as easy as possible to learn and implement.

I believe we, as authors, should stick together and help one another. You my friend aren't the competition. You're just like me. You love writing, and want to share it with the world. That's why I decided to write this book.

Contained within this book, is a culmination of all those techniques and strategies I spent countless hours studying.

I've tried to break them down and make it as simple as possible so that my students – yes you, can write a book, without any formal training, in under a month – GUARANTEED!

You're soon going to learn:

- How to choose a killer topic that sells.
- How to get in the right mind-set so that nothing stops you from writing your book.
- The importance of an outline and blueprint.
- How to write a bestseller.
- How to research in as little time possible, and so much more.

Now I'm quite sure you've had a wealth of different experiences throughout your life, but now you are about to embark on a new adventure – YOU ARE GOING TO WRITE YOUR OWN BOOK. Who knows where this may lead, no doubt it'll be a personal achievement, but it could also be one of the biggest marketing efforts taken on that could lead to unimaginable profits. I, personally hope you do have a massive success with your endeavour. Whatever, the case may be, I'll be here to help you every step of the way.

Just the thought of you implementing the techniques I've acquired and developed over the years fills me with excitement, as I remember the first time I used the techniques, the techniques I still use today.

Before I continue though, I need to tell you that the book you'll be reading and digesting, although complete, is still a work in progress. The reason for this is simply, I'm learning new techniques every day. I continuously strive to find new techniques and strategies that will help me with my writing, however, rest assured it contains all the information you could want to write your book in the fastest time possible. So the book you have in front of you, although current and up to date, might not be in a few months. I'll be constantly making changes, offering improvements and introducing new ideas and strategies to make this book the best it can be and improve on its success.

So, if you haven't already, visit my website **www.simplewritingstrategies.com** and subscribe to my newsletter.

The reason you should subscribe is twofold. By signing up, you'll always receive the latest news and developments in the writing world, just as I receive them, thus giving you free updates for life, so you'll always have up to date techniques and secondly, I hope it will give you the chance to write about your successes as this is a new endeavour for the both of us.

Please don't worry, you're not getting a book that is old and out-dated, you're getting the very latest thoughts and ideas. In many cases, you're reading what I just learnt last week.

I'm going to jump right in with the first strategy. Now this is **important**, so take note. When you begin the actual process of writing, and by that I mean getting your words down onto paper or on your computer screen, forget about spelling and grammar. I know this doesn't make sense and may go against every fibre of your writing being, but hear me out. Spelling and grammatical errors can always be rectified in later versions. This was a mistake I made when I first started out, it took me so long to write my first book that I gave up in the end and it never got finished, because it got lost when I moved. That was over a year of work wasted for nothing.

Please learn from my mistakes and just get the words onto paper; editing can always be done later.

If I waited until the text was perfect, this course would've never been written and I wouldn't be sharing my success with you. Always keep this in mind. **Write first, edit later.**

I also want you to know that the techniques shown for writing a book in under 30 days applies to both fiction and non-fiction. Both can be written at unbelievable speeds. Unfortunately, as you read certain chapters, you'll get the distinct impression I am talking about non-fiction, when you want to write fiction, or vice versa. Please understand, that in nearly every chapter of this book – I'm talking about fiction and non-fiction. In some cases, I might focus on fiction to give you an example, but understand the same technique can also be used for non-fiction. I also delve into techniques like character development, which only relates to fiction, if you are a non-fiction writer, then you may want to skip these parts.

Why should I listen to you? I hear you ask. Well, I have been writing ever since I could hold a pen, I live to write, it's in my blood. I've had many short stories published in various publications. I've held writing workshops over the last few years helping writers and teaching them the same techniques as you are about to learn. Some have had publishing success, while others just write for fun. Now I want to help as many people realise their dream of being a published author too.

Whatever you decide to write, please try the techniques, they have worked for me time and time again and I have started to get students from all over the world having success with these techniques. The only reason you could possibly fail to write your book is that you decide not to use these techniques. You are moments away from learning the best techniques to write, publish and market your book for profit so keep reading.

I look forward to seeing your book in print, and to hearing about your success.

<u>Chapter 1</u>

Why it's imperative to write your book in the shortest time possible and create the greatest ever-marketing tool in your arsenal.

Before we begin on our journey I would like to make a few apologies, so I don't upset anyone. Call it housekeeping if you will. Throughout this book I will be using the masculine pronoun "he" for both genders. It's not because I'm sexist, it's just easier. I'm what you call a lazy writer, if I can say something in the least possible words and still get my message across, I will. You'll also note that when explaining some of the techniques, I will refer to non-fiction. Don't worry, as mentioned in the introduction, these techniques are used for both. It's just far more convenient to use one, than to shuffle back and forth. I hope you understand.

Now that the formalities are out of the way, let us begin...

One of the main reasons I decided to write this book is because a little than a year ago I was looking for more ways to sell my books, I turned to the internet and found Internet Marketing. One day, I attended a conference and met up with a chap called Daniel Wagner. If you are an Internet Marketer, you may know of him. At the time, I didn't know who he was, but what attracted me to him was he was holding a book in his hand. I approached him and introduced myself. After a while, I asked him about the book he was holding, he handed it to me and said it was one of the top reasons he was a successful Internet Marketer. It was his own book – **My Journey and the machine.** If you get a chance, I urge you to read it; it is a great and inspiring read. It was the reason people in the Internet marketing community trusted him, and the reason he had instant credibility with clients and prospects alike.

He went on to explain that as soon as he had the book in his hands, it became an instant and incredibly powerful marketing book for him.

One of the great things about writing your own book is you instantly become an expert in your field and gain instant credibility.

I remember when I published my first novel "Muti". It was all about South African witchcraft. Once people had read it, they would come to me and ask me all sorts of questions on the subject because they believed I was an expert in the field. That's how powerful a book can be and how powerful it will be for you once it's written.

Why creating your book is the greatest ever marketing tool you'll have in your arsenal if you're a professional or consultant.

If someone came up to you on the street and said to you, *"I have a special machine here with me, if you give me £10, it will make £20 for you."* Reluctantly, you hand over the £10, watch the process, seeing that it's totally legitimate, what would you do? My guess is you'll go directly to your bank account and drain it of £10 notes.

Well in a way, that's what you have in front of you right now. You've got a book, a machine that's going to show you how to produce the most powerful marketing tool you or your business will ever encounter. In a matter of weeks you're going to have that marketing tool to bring in more revenue, clients and profits and rocket your career into the stratosphere. You may experience more success than you thought possible.

Your book will be the most important marketing tool in your arsenal because it will give you and your business instant credibility. It sets you apart from every other professional or consultant in your field. It can be turned into a client magnet that attracts leads and puts them right in your lap. What's more, clients will not only buy the book to learn from you, they will trust you enough to be repeat buyers, and that's where the truly massive profits come into play.

Okay – so you're not interested in writing a non-fiction book, you're more into crime dramas.

How would your life be changed if one day you found yourself on Richard and Judy speaking about your new novel, or the Today Show?

What if you enjoyed the success as a published fiction author, with publishers waiting with baited breath for your next novel?

Well, you'll find the same steps I used to write my own novels within the pages of this book. This system has been designed and perfected to help you write your fiction or non-fiction book, in the shortest time possible.

If you want to write fiction, I'm sure you realise the benefits that come with notoriety, but first let's have a look and the benefits of writing a non-fiction book.

How people perceive you when you've written your own book.

Let's look at it from your point of view. Say you attend a seminar and meet someone that has written a book in your field. I'll guarantee you, you think of them as an expert in that field. I immediately thought so of Daniel Wagner. They'll be the person you go to for help. It seems logical as they have had work published in your chosen field. They've been on local radio and T.V, they might even be a celebrity. Just look at the financial guru Robert Kiyosaki, author of **Rich Dad, Poor Dad.** (It's an excellent book, which I recommend you read, just read the reviews he gets.) He has an army of followers eager to hear what he has to say.

They're pretty much convinced that he's going to provide them with the most value when it comes to real-estate investing.

If people, like Robert, are published authors, and are the experts, then it stands to reason that they know more than anyone else, right?

They're knowledge and services, must be worth far more than anyone else's. After all, if it wasn't true, they wouldn't have a book published on the subject, right?

Crikey, it's even in part of our language. We hear the phrase, "He wrote a book on it," all the time. It's used as a saying when we talk about a person that knows an extensive amount on a particular subject. So if you want the right info, the right answers to your questions, then the author who has written a book on your subject must be the one you surely contact!

Going back to Robert Kiyosaki, basically he's done what every other professional wants to do, separated himself from all the other competitors in his field and put himself on the forefront of his prospective customers mind.

And that's what makes writing a book one of the most powerful marketing tools any professional can have.

It creates massive awareness of your skills and gives you a reach no other marketer has. That awareness and credibility can be easily translated into your business to create massive profits.

The author (professional) is the expert. That's how their readers (customers) view them. In the society we live in, if someone publishes a book, it means that the editor or publisher approves of what the author has to say in a book, thus giving instant credibility to it.

Your book is an ultimate testimonial, of you and your business and as we know testimonials are one of the best marketing strategies on the planet. Just think back to when you brought your latest product, I bet deep down you were swayed to purchase from the testimonials left by others.

Let's look at it from a slightly different perspective. Okay, let's say you are looking for someone with knowledge and expertise in beekeeping. There's a good chance you won't check out the latest ads, you may go to the Internet, but there's a high chance you might ask your friends in passing conversation if they can recommend anyone who's a beekeeper, someone who's been doing it for a long time that will be able to teach you. Maybe your friend is a beekeeper, which would make the recommendation even stronger.

The same goes with your book. A prospective client is looking for a recommendation from someone in authority, they want to cut the learning curve and learn from the best. If you have written a book, you instantly become an authority. See where I'm going with this?

Okay, so what has this got to do with fiction writing? Well, when I set about writing my first novel about South African witchcraft and rituals, I needed to find out how to write about the British Criminal system and police procedures. What do you think I did? Yep, you guessed it; I went and brought a book. **"A Writer's Guide to Police Organisation, Crime Investigation and Detection"** by D.J. Cole. I knew I would learn everything I need, because he was an expert in his field. Not only that, I have since brought several of his books.

Then, one day after my book was published, I received an e-mail, it was from a young woman who had brought and read my book, she wanted to know about witchdoctors, as she was writing a paper on the supernatural. Because she read the book, she instantly thought I

was an expert on the subject and wanted to interview me for her paper. So you see it doesn't matter if you're writing fiction or non-fiction, the same rules apply.

In the society we live in, anyone who is a celebrity in a certain field is looked up to. If they're in a position of power, they must know a great deal of what you're interested in.

Just look at all the celebrity chefs, how many people have the chefs' cookbooks on their shelves? Or fitness TV personalities, many people have their own workout videos lining the bookshelves? That's just the way the world works.

So if a publishing company decides to publish your book, or it gets reviewed by a newspaper or on the TV and radio, then you have instantly passed the credibility test. You are now the expert in your field.

The publisher or media has indirectly given your name and your business name as a referral to countless people reading, listening or watching, who may need your help, or indeed, looking for a good read for their holidays.

If you're not getting good results with your current marketing system, then you NEED to write your book immediately!

Your prospective clients see you as an expert. As an accomplished, successful individual, it doesn't matter if you are or not. They perceive you as an expert, therefore you are an expert, and the fact of the matter is, people want to deal with someone that's already successful.

Why your book will be the "key" to unlimited publicity and promotion.

It's a simple fact, the media loves interviewing celebrities.

When you write your book and get it published, you inadvertently, become a celebrity too and start to get all the benefits that go with it.

Let me explain, a good friend of mine wrote a book on how to become a successful trader. He is well known in this specific industry. Not well known outside, but certainly within. Last year I attended a seminar with him. As we approached the hotel, the reception and bellboys didn't know him, that's to be expected.

However, the next day when he walked into the hall where the seminar was taking place, he was accosted by a variety of people, shaking his hand, asking for tips etc. These were people he'd never met in his life. After the seminar we were ushered into the VIP lounge for drinks and were treated like royalty. Many people complemented him on his book and how much it helped them. Furthermore, it was astonishing to see just how many people had referred him to their friends.

That type of publicity is priceless, and pays huge dividends in his business.

If your prospective clients know who you are and respect you, surely you've already minimised your marketing efforts?

In writing your book, you've created a never-ending stream of potential clients who have already verified in their own mind, that you're the expert who can help them the most.

In the same respect, if you've written a novel that a reader has enjoyed, you've opened them to the idea of buying your next one, and the one after that.

So it just makes complete sense to write your book in the shortest possible time.

You obtain instant expert status, your prospective buyers will see you as a trustworthy

person and they will be calling on you, rather than you calling on them.

Yes, there are other ways to market yourself and your business, advertising for one, but that costs money and if you don't do it right, it can cost you a lot of money. You could spend time on free advertising on social media sites like Facebook and Twitter, but that is time consuming and again, if you don't do it correctly, you could be spending hours in front of the computer for nothing.

Your book, however, will keep on bringing them in, month after month, year after year.

When you look at the alternatives, your benefits, costs and long-term value is clear.

If you spend just 30 days producing your book (I know of people that have done it in less than TWO weeks), you'll be harvesting the benefits for months, if not years, to come.

In the next chapter, I'll be discussing the pitfalls writer's face and how to avoid them as well as answering the most common writing questions. I hope you're still with me...

Chapter 2

Answering the most common writing questions, dispelling the myths surrounding book writing, discussing the pitfalls writers face and how you can avoid them.

There are many problems we as writers face every day. One of the most common ones is the dreaded writers block. Luckily for you I've the answer for you that will not only expel any fears of writers block, but will allow you to write your book faster than you ever imagined.

In this chapter I'm going to discuss a few myths surrounding writing as well as answering a few questions you may have already been thinking.

So while this chapter contains the least amount of 'how to' information in the book, it may be the most important.

So let's get to it.

1.) Do I need a professional qualification to write my book?

The simple answer is no, of course not. I'll let you in on a little fact. I don't have any professional writing qualifications; I'm just like you. I didn't spend years at university honing my writing craft. I have to admit though, I did unfortunately, spend a fortune on books, e-books and courses, teaching myself, but to be quite honest, I didn't need to. All I really needed was a couple of really good mentors to show me the way. Now I'd like the opportunity to become your mentor.

You show me a person that says you need a professional qualification to write a book, and I'll show you a liar.

Okay then smarty pants, what qualifications do you need to write your book? I hear you ask.

Well firstly, if you are thinking of writing non-fiction, you need to give the readers the information they need to accomplish their goals. Most buyers of non-fiction books are looking for a solution to a specific problem, whether it is building a shed, losing weight or making money online. This can be new information they don't already have or just a new and fresh perspective on information already out there, a spin on an old idea. For instance, there's a young man that constantly gets bullied at school. He desperately wants to learn how to defend himself. Now lets say you're a martial arts ninja and you've written a book on ninja

moves that can kick bully's butts. My guess is as soon as he sees your book; he'll want to snap it up. If you give as much information about cool ninja moves, then you're on to a winner.

But if I give them all the information they need in the book, they won't need my services anymore! This statement couldn't be further from the truth. The more information you give to your readers, the more likely they are to trust you to become repeat buyers. There are always areas you can expand on or more information the readers want to know.

One of my first rules when it comes to writing non-fiction is give the readers exactly what they want and *always* over deliver.

In fiction terms, a reader wants to be taken from the world they live in, into another world. They want to escape reality, even if it's for a short while. You've got to provide them with an escape to a world that they can engross themselves in. So all you need an active imagination, I'll show you the rest within these pages.

Next comes your commitment. You've got to be 100% committed to helping your readers get the results they are looking for. It doesn't necessarily mean the book has all the answers, you can point out the solution in your book, but if they want to implement what is taught in the book, well then you are in the perfect position to offer a consultation service.

If you're committed to helping your readers get the benefits of what you have to offer, then your book will be a rip-roaring success and you'll be able to exploit this fantastic marketing opportunity. Remember this, your readers are the ones that pay your wage. Help them with their problem and they'll pay you handsomely for it. Leave them feeling cheated, then you have lost that reader and the money they would've spent on you.

2.) What if I can't think of anything to say?

Now I find that this can be one of the biggest challenges facing writers today, especially non-fiction writers. In fact when I started out, I was in the exact same position. I had an idea but that was about it. My problem was I thought that whatever I came up with, it had been done before. I lacked the ability to say something new or different, thus distinguishing myself from the pack.

However, as I soon learnt, simply using the information I had already gathered over the years and putting it in my own words was sufficient enough. Getting the basics out into your book is the first step to your success.

Look at it from this perspective, say you have bred and kept Iguana's as a hobby since you were a child. In the beginning, you picked up books and learnt from them, right? Yet, over the years you've been developing your own techniques, on the best way to breed and keep them alive. Each way is unique to you. So I have no doubt that the knowledge you pass on to your reader will contribute to their success as an iguana breeder. Basically, start with what you know and the rest will follow with a little research.

Then, of course, there's creativity. This next little trick is something that I continue to use to get my creative juices flowing, and something you too, should always try to implement when you get stuck. Anyone can expand on the knowledge already out there by simply asking "what if". *What if we did that? What if we didn't do that? What if we took that out and put this in?* See where I'm going with this?

When you expand on the knowledge out there, you've gone beyond what is commonly known and distinguished yourself in your chosen field.

If you're ever stuck for something to write, remember these two words MIND POWER. Think of the mind as a very powerful computer. You can ask it almost anything and sure enough with a bit of creative thinking and research, you'll probably find an answer. There's more ideas in your niche or particular field than you could have thought possible, all you have to do is train your mind to "think out the box" to start seeing the results you require.

Helping you develop your ideas, to pull them from the recesses of your mind until a tsunami of ideas come flooding through for the benefit of your readers, will be my job.

Stick with me and I'll show you just how easy it can be.

What if I can't write? I am here to tell you, you can. Anyone can, and it's another reason why it's imperative you write your book now.

If you can write a letter or and e-mail – heck just put pen to paper, regardless of the technique, then there is as many books inside you as there are ideas.

You started to learn to write when you started school, you continued to write throughout your schooling, yet somewhere along the way, you tell yourself it's hard, that you need years of hard studying to perfect your writing. I'm here to tell you there is nothing further from the truth. Look back to when you were a kid, writing was fun, and easy, nothing has changed, just your mindset. With my help I will break down the walls of insecurity and get you writing like a speed demon in no time.

As for creativity, you may not know it, but I believe you have it, in bucket-loads. Just the mere fact that you have brought this book has told me you have it in you.

When I first starting teaching these very same techniques you're about to discover to my writing class, I easily proved that they could develop at least a dozen story ideas in a few minutes.

Your writing talent could be limitless, if you learn the art of effective writing.

You'll need to learn to take a non-critical approach to your writing. This is imperative if you want to succeed as a writer. If you are a perfectionist, getting hung up on the little things, then I'm afraid you'll never finish your work. If you have any self-doubt, this will surely hinder your writing and will inevitably discourage you. Remember what I said about mind power? Just think of yourself as the greatest writer that ever lived and sure enough, your writing will flourish.

One of my strategies I have developed over the years, thanks to a few of my mentors, is to write as fast as you can, without thinking too much or going back to edit as you go along.

You'll notice that I will speak a lot about this strategy throughout this book, as it is the premise to good writing: the faster you write, the better you write. Sounds strange, but you'll see it works like a charm.

Another valuable tip I learnt over the years is never, ever, under any circumstances write when you're tired. If you're tired, your brain is telling you, you need sleep. The last thing it wants to do is writing. If you write tired, your writing will suffer.

3.) Won't the book be of poor quality if I write fast?

This is a question I hear a lot, and every time I answer it, just like it was answered to me when I first asked the very same question: 'There's no relationship between the amount of time you spend on something and the inherent quality or value within it.'

However, people naturally assume the longer you take to create something, the more value and higher quality it will be.

In fact Robert Louis Stevenson's **"The strange case of Dr. Jekyll and Mr. Hyde"** was produced in only 72 hours, and that is a masterpiece that is as popular today, as it was when it was first published in 1886. Arthur Conan Doyle's **"A Study in Scarlett"** about Sherlock

Holmes first adventure was written in 3 weeks again in 1886. However, Charles Dickens's **"A Christmas Carol"** took a little longer, and was completed in 6 weeks in 1843.

So do yourself a favour, when you have completed your book in under a month, just tell people it took you years to create and they'll instantly see the quality in your work.

4.) How can I create real literary value?

If you want your book to have long-term value, it has to be reader focused. It must have everything your readers need to solve their problem to get the results they require. That means no holding back, always over deliver and make sure they walk away thinking they got true value. If you skimp on this strategy, then your readers will know and your business and reputation will suffer for it.

Fill your book with as many benefits to the reader as you can, when you've crammed as much useful information for the reader as you can into your book, then you know you have created real literary value.

You need to always present solutions to the reader's problems. They don't buy books because they like to spend money, they buy it because they want to study and benefit from the solutions you've supplied to their problems. In non-fiction, the reader judges the book on the results they get based on the information you present. In fiction, it's a little different but the same rules still apply. You need to give them twists and turns, ups and downs. You need to take them on such a thrilling roller-coaster ride of emotions that when they finish reading your book, they must be left with such a sense of excitement, so that they just can't wait until the next one comes out.

In the end, your book's quality will be judged on these points.

Before I continue, I'd like to make it clear, that writing a book in under a month **doesn't include the research aspect or editing.** Rest assured though, will be covering these topics to minimise the time spent on each discipline.

So you don't just learn how to write a book in under a month, it's a lot more.

5.) This all sounds great but I want to write fiction!

You're not alone, I, at heart, am a fiction writer, so I can relate. Remember, I used the exact same strategies as you are going to learn to write my novels.

Like I mentioned earlier, all the techniques and strategies mentioned in this book are tailored to both. Just think of the reasons for buying a book. For the non-fiction readers, it's the information they need to solve a problem, for the fiction readers, it's a fantastic story.

This book covers both. If there are differences, I'll let you know.

6.) I just don't have the time to write a book.

This is by far one of the most annoying excuses I hear. You've more than enough time, believe me. All the writers of both fiction and non-fiction, who've used their books to advance their own careers, stick to the same rules governed by time as you and I. They have the exact same hours in the day as you do. (Unless one mad scientist writer has discovered time travel and isn't telling the rest of us.) The difference is, they block out the time needed to write their book. From here on in, you need to adopt the same attitude. Instead of watching TV, or playing video games, sit in front of the computer and get writing.

If you schedule an hour or so every day, just like I do, your book will be completed in no time at all.

If you need any motivation, write this down and make sure you can see it everyday as a reminder. **This book is going to boost your career, open new doors, enable you to quit that job you hate so much and be your own boss.** So think of it as this: A job you need to complete that will help others as well as yourself.

The next problem regarding time is that you think you need at least a few hours to do anything significant when it comes to writing. Again, this is a complete farce. With the techniques you'll discover in this book, you'll need no more than 5 minutes for your book to advance significantly.

If you can spare five minutes in your lunch break, waiting for your partner to finish work, then you've more than enough time to write your book.

It's possible and I'll show you how.

7.) I don't have any writing ability!

Err – wrong again. If you can talk, you can write. If you write letters or e-mails to friends, then you can write. Absolutely everyone has a writing ability.

Good writing is just the literary version of good talking. If you have something of interest to say, then you have something of interest to write.

My main rule for writing is write the way you talk. Any time you read something that is bad, it's because the words don't sound if someone is actually speaking them.

One thing that bugs the hell out of me is most writers always want to sound sophisticated when they write, so they use big words that aren't usually used in common speech. I don't know about you, but this frustrates me, as I have to haul out the dictionary to find out what they mean. Today it's a bit easier with the invention of e-readers like the Kindle that have in built dictionaries, but for those people that still like the feel and smell of a book, it can be quite annoying. So unwittingly, the writer is actually moving away from good

writing, because not only does the reader not understand the message the writer wants to put across, it interrupts the flow of the book.

Which swiftly brings me nicely on to the next point. When writing, try to use simple language. Don't use big words to try and sound sophisticated and intelligent because you'll lose half, if not more, of your readers. Here's a quick tip to keep in mind.

Those educated folks who understand the big words, understand the small ones too. However, simpletons like me who only understand the small words, get the message if you use only small words.

If you write the way you talk, you will write well. Also the faster you do something, usually, the better you do it. If you write quickly, you write the way you talk, which means you'll be writing well.

One of the best ways I like to write is if I imagine talking to a friend. If I envision my best friend sitting there right next to me, and I'm chatting away to him.

8.) I don't have clear direction!

I find direction can be a big problem for writers. They don't know where they're going, so they never know if they're headed in the right direction.

This means, that books with no direction are, at best, a series of paths with a few detours here and there, that ultimately, lead to nowhere.

So, how do you get direction? First, you need a good, interesting topic. If you have that, then you have an excellent starting point. It also comes down to focus, if you know what your book will be about before you've written it, you can focus on the essential elements and have a clear path you would like your book to take.

Remember, if you're writing non-fiction, you need to have a solution to your reader's problem. That's why they've brought the book in the first place, they're looking for a solution to their problem, whether it's to lose weight, stop smoking or build muscle. If you can give them a detailed account of how they can solve their problem, then you will have a customer eager for your next book.

For fiction, you've got to have a winning story or plot. Something that will grab your reader by the collar, lead them down an entertaining path, leading them right where you want them to be.

If you follow my simple strategies contained within this book, you'll know the entire manuscript before you've even written it.

9.) I don't have any deadlines set to complete my book.

I believe deadlines are instrumental and one of the essential ingredients for success. The deadline, in my opinion, makes a person productive, and I'm sure I'm not the only one that thinks this.

If you don't believe me, then think back to the last time you had someone over for a surprise visit. You knew they about to arrive in just under a half an hour and the place was a tip. Chances are you cleaned the house like you were possessed.

The same is in writing, the closer I get to a deadline, the more productive I become, and my writing flows faster than a raging torrent.

My aim is for you to take full advantage of this fact. I urge you to write to five-minute deadlines. If you do this and write to the five-minute deadline, you are guaranteed to be productive.

My average is about 250 words every five minutes, believe me, I don't type fast, I'm what you call a two-finger typist. So you'll soon see that typing to five minute deadlines is not only productive, you'll finish your book in the fastest time possible.

10.) I'm not really clear on my topic.

This goes hand in hand with not being focused.

You'll be writing a response to a problem a reader has, or an entertainment need. You'll have to identify the problem, and then work toward solving that problem, or need, for the reader. If you don't know the problem, here's what I like to do. Firstly I like to go to Amazon and look at the best sellers. If there is a need for it and people are buying books on your related topic, then you have an idea what readers' problems are. I would then go to Yahoo Answers and look to see if people are asking questions about my topic, if there are a lot of questions on the same topic, then you know a lot of people are looking for answers to their problems. Then you could just go flat out and ask your potential readers, ask them to complete a survey for a free gift, more often than not, they will tell you their concerns, and then you can work toward offering them a solution. You can find them on forums, and social media sites like Facebook. The same goes for fiction, just ask what the reader wants in their ideal novel, and work to create it for them.

Remember this when writing your book. Keep it simple. Simple answers are easier to remember.

11.) But I don't have the motivation to write my book.

When I first started writing, this is something I battled with constantly, as with many other writers. Luckily, over the years, thanks to my mentors, I have adapted a technique I call the "Winning Writing Machine". I have tried to make this technique as simple as possible so you don't need to get motivated to write your book. If you still need motivation after using this technique, it's because you don't have goals, or your goals aren't strong enough for you to succeed. You'll need to revise your goals and visualise what the benefits will be after you've written your book and got it published.

Think of it this way, your book is a key that is going to open many doors. It's your ticket to your success and everything that comes with it, notoriety, fame and fortune.

When you've got that kind of insight and hold on to it, motivation is easy.

12.) I don't have the talent to write my book.

To be good at your chosen career or profession, you need a certain amount of talent to be successful.

Writing, however, is something totally different. I believe that writing requires little or no talent whatsoever. Are you talented because you can speak? Not really – so if you write the way you talk, then by definition, you don't need to be talented. I believe people with writing "talent" always get bogged down with writing stunning prose. You don't want that for your book, the more time you spend on making your prose perfect, the longer it will take to write your book, and the more time you have for self-doubt to creep in.

What you want is clear, concise thinking, a step-by-step, and easy to follow solution, to the reader's problem.

This happens when you write as quickly as possible. Simply write down the words as the flow from your mind.

Fiction writing, however, demands a little more talent, call it more of an active imagination, but if you can get the words flowing from your mind onto the paper, you'll be pleasantly surprised how competent you can be as a writer.

13.) I keep getting stumped by writer's block.

Wow, if I had a penny every time a writer complained of the dreaded 'writer's block', I would be sitting on a beach somewhere sipping cocktails, watching the sun go down over the beautifully tranquil sea.

To me, writers cause writer block themselves. It's like an excuse for them not to pick up a pen to write. They stare at the page blankly; they don't know where to take the plot next. To me this is down to the lack of planning. It only arises when the writer doesn't know what to write next.

If you plan an 'outline' of a book so you know exactly where the book is going to go from start to finish, then you'll not have a problem with writer's block. Luckily for you, I'm going to teach you exactly how to create a fantastic outline so you'll never struggle for words.

14.) I'm uncertain, I don't think I'm worthy of the task.

Stop right there and banish any thought that you're unworthy. If you have a story to tell or if you can provide a solution to a problem, then my friend, you are worthy of writing your book. Besides, if other people were more worthy than you, how come they haven't written one? If you're sincere about helping others, then you have what it takes to be a writer. Those around you want to learn, and you have the information and tools (your book) they need. If you wait before you "know it all" before you write you book, then I'm afraid it will never happen.

No one, and I mean no one, knows everything on their topic. That person just doesn't exist. So start with what you've got and what you know.

15.) I don't know where to start.

When people ask me this I always say this: "Start at the most interesting point." For crime writers it's usually a murder being committed, for romance novelists, it could be a flashback when the hero met the love of his life. As for non-fiction writers I find a good starting point is telling the reader why you've decided to write your book and how it will benefit them. If you don't know what the most interesting point is, jot a few ideas down on a piece of paper and then eliminate them one by one X Factor style until you have one, then go from there. The good thing about this technique, you know pretty much what to say next because you have the ideas jotted down in front of you.

Remember this important fact. Your reader wants to be grabbed and pulled into the story immediately. They don't want to wait until page 20 before it starts to get good, by that time, they would've put the book down and gone onto another one. So you need to grab their attention with the first sentence, hell the first paragraph. So if you don't want to lose a valuable reader, you better start off with the most exciting point.

16.) I have no idea on how to finish it.

This, to me, seems like a silly idea. The whole point of writing a book is to –well, write a book. If you don't have a finish in mind then you could end up with a book 900 pages long and still not be finished.

Your finishing point must be a complete solution to the specific problem you're writing about, or a successful conclusion to the story. It's not designed to be the answers of all the questions in the universe.

You simply want it to answer the question it was designed for, nothing more, and nothing less.

I'll be showing you a very special technique that will allow you to "see" your entire manuscript before it's even written, so the idea of not knowing how to finish it will become obsolete. Carry on reading and you'll soon find it out.

17.) There's too much research to do.

There's no doubt that research is a vital ingredient to a successful book, whether you are writing fiction or non-fiction, you want it to be believable for the reader, otherwise you may end up losing a repeat customer. You need all the facts before writing your book.

However, in saying that, many writers get stuck in the "research trap" and find themselves researching far too much. They find themselves researching one bit, only to find it has opened several other areas that need to be researched.

There is a very simple solution to this problem. **Just stop.** Before you set off on your research mission, you need to know exactly what you're looking for, and that's it.

The most important part of your research is that you know what you're looking for, the second is to understand that everything else is irrelevant and isn't needed in your book.

When you get to the research section in this book, I'll show you how to do the minimum amount of research in the shortest possible time. Yes, research is an important part of your book, but not the most. If you don't get stuck on research, you have more time for writing, and for me, that it the most important part, getting it done.

18.) But I'm a perfectionist.

Now I'm not a violent man, but whenever I hear those words uttered by a writer, I just want to punch them in the face.

I must apologise, but I am going to give you some hard truths now. If you're a perfectionist and get hung up on spelling, grammar, prose and the rest, I am afraid to say your book will **never** be finished. You'll accomplish nothing, create nothing and perfect nothing. Nothing is ever perfect, and it never will be. If you ever get your book published, then it will be imperfect, so you may as well resign yourself to that fact now, as soon as you do, you can carry on with the essential part of the process – writing your book.

If your book gets published with a few flaws in it, well, welcome to the club.

In fact, you want it to be imperfect. You want to leave the reader begging for more, you can always address some issues you left out of your book in your next one.

So stop trying to write the perfect book, because it will never happen and you'll never get your book finished otherwise.

Conclusion.

You may think it's hard, or you need specific qualifications or you just can't write your book. I'm here to tell you, you can. It's really not as hard as you think. Hell, if a yokel like me can write a book, then you certainly can. Let me tell you this, if you think you can't write a book, then someone else, probably less qualified than you, will write it for you. Don't let that happen, you owe it to yourself and your reader to get it written.

In chapter 3 I'm going to talk a little more in depth about getting in the right mindset, so that absolutely nothing will stop you from producing a best seller. See you there.

<u>Chapter 3</u>

Learning how to get in the right mindset. So that nothing will distract you from writing your book.

Motivating yourself to get your book written does play a part of the writing book strategy, so I'm going to mention it here briefly. I say only briefly because getting in the right mindset and having the right positive attitude, to me, is more important. But for now, let me just say a few words about motivation. One of the easiest ways I motivate myself to write books is by visual stimulation. Whatever your reasons are for writing your book, jot them down on a piece of paper and stick it somewhere you can see it every day. For example, my motivation for writing this book was to help others realise their dream to see their own book in print. So, I wrote that down on a piece of paper, along with several other factors and stuck it on the fridge. Every time I went for a snack, it was there, spurring me on. I suggest you do the same, I promise, constantly seeing the reminder **will** spur you on.

Now I want to discuss the importance of having the right mindset before you start writing. There's no difference between a person that has written a book to one that hasn't (except for the obvious). The author has written one, the non-author has not. It's that simple.

In saying that, a person that has written one book, can go on to write several or even several dozen. There's nothing to say that you'll "dry out," that you've no more gas in the tank. The brain is a wonderful thing and as long as you can think, you can write books. All you have to do is open your mind to the possibility. As soon as you acknowledge that there're hundreds of books within you, then the possibilities become limitless.

Now don't get me wrong, I'm not implying that all you have to do is "think" you can write a book and it will miraculously happen. All I'm trying to get across is that you must realise that there's no doubt in your mind it's possible, and you'll never have enough time in the world to produce them all.

How to slay the monster that is procrastination.

If you're ever to succeed in writing your book, you must get rid of procrastination. So many times I have heard the line, "I'll do it tomorrow", only to find that when tomorrow comes, you find another excuse not to write your book. You must banish this from your mind. My writing techniques can do this to a certain extent, but I cannot be there by your side spurring you on, this is something you have to tackle on your own.

Think of all the things you could've achieved over the years, how far you could've gone in your career if it wasn't for procrastination. If you are not where you envisioned yourself to be in your life or career, realise it's because of procrastination.

Now here's the cold hard truth about procrastination, no one but yourself cares if you procrastinate. Not your friends, your family, your colleagues or even me, we all don't care if you procrastinate or not. Only you feel the effects of your own procrastination, so the sooner you kick it to touch, the sooner you can get on with the things you want to do in life.

And if that doesn't help you, send me an e-mail at **procrastination@simplewritingstrategies.com** with the subject header: "help me with my procrastination", and I'll happily send you a free e-book on the subject that helped me when I was in the same position.

Tapping into the well of unlimited ideas.

Although you may not realise it, but you have a wealth of ideas, stories and possibilities in your mind right now. You may think that you have only one idea, and when that idea is exhausted, you have nothing left. Take a look around you, all you have to do is open your eyes to the possibilities and they'll come flooding in. One way I get ideas from my novels is going to my local park and "ear wigging" on other people's conversations, you'll be amazed at how many stories you can think of. Pick up a newspaper, we read stories every day. Talk to people, find out what they want, what they need. All you have to do is write a few ideas on a piece of paper and use the techniques written in this book. Once you realise there isn't a limit to the ideas you can create in books, there'll be no limit to the amount of books you can write for your readers.

Why having a strategy is the best thing for your book.

Have you ever baked a cake? If you have, you'll know there's a vital ingredient you need for its success, and that's a recipe. If you follow that recipe, you'll always bake a cake, you'll never end up with scones or bread, it will always be a cake.

Writing is similar, if you want to create a best seller time and time again, then you'll need a strategy.

Now I don't want to quash your creativity here, I'm just trying to make your book into a great book for all to enjoy.

I know an author that wrote his first book and it was a complete success, the critics and readers raved about it, his second book was a complete disaster, his third was readable and his fourth was another bestseller. When interviewing him, I asked him if he had a certain strategy he used when writing, and it wasn't a surprise when he said he hadn't, in fact he had no idea how his first book was a success and the other two that followed weren't.

Some authors just have it, like a master baker who knows his ingredients in his head. People like Dean Koontz, Patricia Cornwall, Terry Pratchett and Steven King. They just produce one bestseller after another. And one thing they have in common? They all have a strategy.

I'll be showing you a strategy that you can use to profit every time.

The need for speed. Four simple steps at becoming a great writer.

Along the way, you'll see that I'll be repeating myself quite a bit. The reason for this is because it's an important part of the strategy and will help you become a strong and good writer, capable of producing great work.

Step one: Always write in a simple and straightforward style. I gleaned this from an article I read about one of the most prolific writers of our time, Isaac Asimov, the science fiction writer. In the interview, the interviewer asked him why he was prolific, what caused him to have such a wealth of good writing? His answer, in my opinion, is useful to both budding and veteran writers alike. **'I guess I'm prolific because I have a simple and straightforward style,'** he said.

You need to drill that statement into your mind. To be prolific, you need a simple and straightforward style.

Let me explain a little better. I bet that you know someone that does something really well. Chances are, because they do it so well, they do it quickly too. The reason for this is because they've done it so often, they've mastered the technique, process and challenges. With this mastery comes proficiency, and proficiency is always accompanied by speed.

On to **step two**, if you want to write well, write the way to talk. If you write the way you talk, you'll always be understandable to your reader and they won't get lost in translation. If you write the way to talk, there'll be no convoluted sentences, no misunderstanding and no misinterpretation.

When you're chatting to your friends, you don't "put on airs" in your speech, unless it's to attract the opposite sex, then again, that can backfire if they don't understand you. You speak to be understood. Just about every agent, editor, publisher and reader will tell you that if you write the way you talk, your manuscript will be more readable, publishable and more importantly, sellable.

Since you were a child, you were able to talk, by now you're a master of speech, use that to your advantage. You have mastered the technique, process and challenges of speech, with this mastery comes proficiency and with proficiency comes speed. Sound familiar?

You talk quickly because you've mastered the art of speech. You know what you want to say and how to say it. Those who know how to do something well, do it quickly, so by that inescapable logic, if you want to write well, write the way you talk. If you want to write well, write quickly. If you write quickly, you will always write the way you talk and you won't have the time to create any awkward sentences.

It can be broken down as follows:

If you want to write well, write quickly.
If you want to be prolific, write quickly,

The faster you write, the better you write.

A perfect example of this is the late Barbara Cartland. She produced a book every week or so, while she was writing. You'd think that writing a book at that speed wouldn't produce anything of value, yet her readers find her books most enjoyable. If you've ever read any of her books, you'll know that her style was so simplistic it's almost laughable. She knew exactly what would happen in each book because she had a strategy that had been ingrained by the many years of reading and writing. She also wrote as she talked, literally. She employed three stenographers she dictated to. Each would take turns in taking dictation and then transcribing it.

Step three, omit needless words. Nearly every editor on this blue planet of ours will agree, if you want you're writing to be powerful, get rid of needless words. If you write the way you talk, you'll write quickly, and if you write quickly, you'll omit needless words.

Now on to the final step, **step four!** If you have a plan (a blueprint or outline), then you'll know exactly what you want to write about every step of the way.

With an outline, you can produce a book in record time. I'll be showing you exactly how to do this later on.

Now it's up to you...

Sadly, there's going to be a lot of people that reading these pages that ARE NOT going to write their book. Despite all the information I've given you, despite all the information that's yet to come, you still may not actually get down to the process of writing your book.

I want you to realise that you must *want* to write your book, I can give you all the tools you need to write your book in the fastest time possible, in fact the strategies and techniques in this book allows it to practically write itself, however, if you aren't willing to write it, then I can't do anything about it.

So you need some sort of motivation or ambition to write it, it doesn't have to be earth shattering, just something that will make you write it, or else sadly, it won't be written.

Know why you want to write your book and know this, that in under a month, possibly a lot sooner, you can have a finished book in your hands.

Commit to writing every day. This can be five, ten, or twenty minutes, it doesn't matter how long, just remain persistent and consistent. Don't skip a single day, if you do, it just makes it easier to skip a second day and a third, and before you know it, months have passed and you still haven't written your book.

It doesn't matter what time of day you write, I prefer the quiet solitude of the night to write, you may prefer early mornings. Whatever the case may be, block out some time to write, even if for a few minutes. You'll soon see you book begin to take shape. Remember what I said in the last chapter, once you decide to write, don't write tired. If you're tired, stop and continue after you're refreshed.

In the next chapter I'm going to be talking about selecting a winning topic that you're readers will pay over the odds for. Stay tuned...

Chapter 4

How to select the killer topic that keeps your readers coming back for more.

Choosing the correct topic for your book is of paramount importance. It could mean the success or failure of your book and here's why.

Your topic must fulfill the two most important desires of your reader, what they want and what they need. What they want is more important than what they need, but both must be given to them in your book. I can't stress this point enough. You could have produced the most beautifully written book, but if it's not what the reader wants, then it's dead in the water and guess what? The publisher won't want to touch it either. Even if you self-publish it, it will be exceedingly hard to sell.

If you can pump out books that your clients want, then you have the key to unlimited success.

Take this book for instance, the reason you brought it is because you *want* to learn how to write a book in under a month. If I wrote this on how to fly-fish in your underpants, you wouldn't want to buy it, would you?

All successful authors have books that are focused on what their readers want. So you need to focus on selecting the right topic for your customers and potential customers. Picking the wrong one only leads to hours of hard work with little reward.

A simple way to pick a great selling topic!

The first thing you need to realise is, no matter what you do in your professional life, your topic can be anything. Sure is helps if you're a photographer and you write about photography, but it's not essential. That same photographer can write a book on skin diving. With the correct amount of research, you can write a book on anything. Don't limit yourself to what you know. The sooner you realise this, the sooner you'll be successful.

The selection of your topic has nothing to do with your abilities and everything to do with your reader.

With that said, ask yourself a simple question. If I could give my readers anything their heart's desired, what would they really want? Think hard, all of your normal constraints have been lifted. You're now free to choose absolutely anything.

It's always good practice keep your readers interests at heart. Ask yourself, what will they benefit from reading my book?
The more desperate a reader is to find a solution to a problem, the better you have a chance of selling your book. I'll give you an example. A man has just been separated from his wife. She blames the break up because of his weight gain. He desperately wants to lose weight so he can get back with his wife. You have a book on how to lose weight quickly. What are the chances he'll snap your hands off to get hold of that book? Pretty great I'm sure you'll agree. If you find a solution to your reader's problems and give them what they want, you'll never have a problem selling your book.

You've just got to believe that you can create anything your heart's desire; all that's required is a little time, effort and research. When you have that self-belief that anything is possible and get rid of your limitations, your imagination runs wild.

How to make sure you have a winning topic.

One way to do this is first come up with a list of about 10 topics or so that you think might interest your readers and prospective readers.

Then ask them, out of the chosen topics, could they chose one they would like to see in print and would be of benefit to them. Once you have a clear winner. That's the topic you should write your book on.

Another way is to do the same thing, pick a few topics, but instead of asking your clients, get online to forums and ask them to choose, or ask your twitter followers or Facebook friends. Just make sure they are interested in the topic and it will be beneficial to them if you write a book on that topic.

But what if you don't have a lot of clients, Facebook friends or people that follow you on twitter?

Forums are a great way to find out what people want. Sign up and let people know in a post that you are doing research for a book and you'll soon see some will be more than happy to have a quick chat. Next you want to find out exactly what they need, they'll tell you that as well. After finding out what they need and want, dig a little deeper, find out the reason why they want something. As I mentioned before it could be a guy wants to lose weight to get his wife back. The more detailed your responses are, the more likely you'll have enough ammo to write a second and a third book. Finally tabulate your responses and find out what the majority of your potential clients want. That will be your topic. Anything else and you'll just be wasting your time.

One final way to make sure you pick a winning topic is search on Amazon. All you need to do is find out what books are selling well, the more demand there is for a book, the more of a need there is for it. Don't worry about competition; in fact, competition is good. More competition means more eyeballs. If you find a plethora of best-selling books on your topic, then you know it's a good market to get into.

As a point of reference and from experience, you can't go wrong with the following topics:

- Weight Loss

- Diet & Weight loss
- Cook books (both diet and non diet)
- Exercise & fitness
- Healthy eating.
- Make money from home
- Dog training
- Erotica
- Children's Books

Creating a topic that gets your readers buzzing with excitement.

You can create a topic that your readers simply won't be able to resist by addressing their biggest need. Sit back and think of your own biggest need at the moment. Have you got something in mind? Fantastic, now picture a book sitting in front of you, the title reads: *"Five easy steps to get* (Insert you need here) *in the shortest possible time without breaking the bank.*

There you have it, a book that you can't resist because it's going to give you exactly what you want. The book title is just as important as the book itself. Get this right and you'll instantly have a new customer before they've even opened the book. Always make sure to tell the reader exactly what they will be getting, by addressing their need in the title of the book. Think of the reason you brought this book. My guess is you brought this because you wanted to learn how to write a profitable book in the shortest possible time. Now look at my title, did it tell you exactly what you wanted to learn? Hmm, I think it did.

This brings me quite nicely onto my next point. Always focus on one topic only. You simply can't please everyone and give everyone what they want. If you focus on more than one topic it dilutes the integrity of the book and the message you're trying to get across. Besides have you ever read a book that helps you stop smoking, lose weight, trade in forex and get through a messy divorce all at once? Of course not! The steps that must be taken to get the benefit the book promises must be easy to implement. Don't make your readers jump through hoops or work out impossible puzzles, it's got to be do-able.

The never-ending topic machine!

Once you've written a book that addresses the customer's needs what then? Have you exhausted that topic? I don't think so. Ask yourself, what's the next logical step? For instance, you wrote a book on losing weight by dieting and your readers loved it. What's the next logical step from there? Surely it will be to write one about getting fit, doing exercises to keep the weight off, right? Then what about writing a book about losing weight after giving birth, then a cookbook with delicious low fat recipes?

Alternatively, you get feedback off your first book. Some people could be having trouble with the theory aspect of the book, maybe it would be a good idea to bring out a workbook for the readers to follow that compliments your first book.

Or you find that after you've written your first book, you still have a plethora of ideas on the same topic you didn't have chance to put in the first one. Just write another one with the words "More of" in front of the title.

Once you open your mind to these possibilities, the ideas will come flooding in and you'll find you'll be easily writing up to two or three books on the same topic, or you title Volume II.

Creating recognition by piggy backing on the success of others!

One way of almost guaranteeing a books success is by capitalising on an already successful book. You can do this by using a variation on the successful book name. It's already had the recognition it deserves, so if you have a book with a similar name, shebang! Instant recognition for you my friend! Remember this. You cannot copyright a title, so you don't have to worry about the legalities of it all. It's a cheap and effective way to get the recognition you wouldn't normally get.

Another way is to get endorsements of other writers or credible people. The more people you can get the better. If you have people saying how wonderful your book is, it makes it easier for your prospective buyers to hand over their hard earned cash for it. It's not really difficult to get an endorsement and it's free. I'll be telling you exactly how to do this a little later in the book.

Creating instant credibility for yourself and your book!

One of the constant questions I get asked is, don't you need to know a lot about your topic before you can write about it? In an ideal world, yes it would be great, but it's really not that necessary. With the creation of the Internet now, it's very easy to research any topic your heart's desire.

Nowadays people aren't looking for qualifications when they buy and read a book, they want results. If you're qualified, then by all means state it in your book, but if you don't have any, simply remain silent and let your book do the talking.

Just by writing the book, you've given yourself instant credibility, and not the credibility that makes the book.

Become the world foremost authority on any topic even if you don't know that much about it.

The main aim of writing your book is to become the foremost authority on your chosen topic. You want to be the person people to go to when they need answers. In the next few paragraphs I'm going to show you exactly how to do that, even if you have a limited amount of knowledge on that subject.

Right, first decide what field of expertise you want to be in. Try to be precise as possible. For instance, if its weight loss try and narrow it down to something like weight loss for new mothers, or weight loss for middle-aged men.

Next get a piece of paper or open a new document on your computer and list all the things you definitely know on the subject. If you don't know anything, don't worry.

Next make a list of all the things you "think" you know on the subject. Just thinking about this might spark something inside you never thought you knew.

After that, make a list of all the things, subjects or facts you definitely don't know. These are the things you should know if you want to be called an expert on that particular topic.

Now what you need to do is make a list of the ten leading experts in that field. If you don't know any experts, pick up any book on the subject and see who wrote it.

Now all you need to do is read the book and digest the information so that it is readily available at your fingertips. What I would recommend is get a notepad and take down notes as you read the books.

Now you're the 11th leading authority on the subject. Time to become number one! Take a look at what you have and simplify it. If you simplify it, made it understandable, you glean it off every other expert out there. You become the only one in the field who has this new, understandable information. Now all you need to do is share it with the world and you will be the world's foremost authority on the subject.

I've spoke a lot on ideas on how to get topics for non-fiction books, you can use the same ideas for fiction, but further on in the book you'll find I talk more in depth about the countless ways to get fiction ideas and concepts. So for the fiction writers out there keep reading.

In chapter 5, things start to heat up in the kitchen. I'm going to go through some of the strategies I use to write a book faster than you ever thought possible. So hold on to your seat belts folks, the ride's about to get interesting.

Chapter 5

Mastering the art of writing your book in under a month. All you need to know to make it happen at lightning speed.

Now we're getting to the exciting stuff. Contained within this chapter is the outline of the main techniques I use to write a book in under a month.

Some of you will write it even faster. Believe me when I say that some of my students have written a book in 2 weeks. Yes, that's not a misprint. I meant to say **TWO weeks**. I'm a typical two-finger typist, so it takes me a little longer to get the words onto the page.

The problem I come across almost daily is that when I say a book can be written in under a month, people laugh at me. They say it can't be done. I'm here to tell you it can, and not only that, soon you'll have the proof. All you need to do is simply take the information I'm going to provide in this chapter and the next few, and put it into practice. This folks, is the very basis of speedwriting.

I'm mentioning this again and will continue to mention it, as the techniques are the very core of the speedwriting process. Remember this lesson well.

If we write the way we talk, we will write quickly. If we write quickly, we'll be prolific writers. If we're prolific and write quickly, we'll inevitably write in a simple and straightforward style, a style any reader will be able to understand. Moreover, if we write the way we talk and write quickly, we will avoid the use of unnecessary words. The faster we write, the better we write.

Learn to write as fast as you can, (I'll be showing you how) Once you can write as fast as you can talk, which thanks to modern technology, is possible, you're writing extremely well and you're prolific. You could be easily writing 12 books a year.

The faster you write, the better you write, which makes your writing read as if you're talking directly to the reader, and that my friend, is the most powerful writing style of all.

Many people are reluctant to accept this concept. It's been drilled into us that for your work to be good, you have to spend hours editing, getting it perfect. This is how we've been traditionally taught. This couldn't be further from the truth.

Great writing comes from when we write the way we talk, and when you write the way you talk, you write quickly. Quantity and quality go hand in hand, as you'll soon see.

Why constantly asking yourself questions helps you to write faster than you ever thought possible.

If I asked you to write about the computer you have, you'll be hard pressed to write a few sentences. This is completely normal. Going on the basis that we write the way we talk, if you were talking about the computer, you'll stop every now and again, thinking of what next to say, getting the order of your words right.

However, if I were to pose it as a question, for example: why does your computer help you with your daily life? I bet you'll be able to write at least two-thirds of a page. I call this, the writer's response.

The reason for this is, we're always able to write a response to a specific question, but we find it hard to write a response to a statement. If you cast your mind back to when you were in school, you could always write a good response when you were asked a question. But when you reached university and had to do a dissertation, you found it much harder to write. That is just the way we're programmed to function.

Let me give you a brief example: A good friend of mine is a PE teacher, at the end of year he has the job of commenting on his student's report cards. Even though each student is different, he finds he starts leaving the same comments for each student.

To avoid this scenario, I told him to think of five questions for each student. How do they interact with others? How do they behave in class? And how did they achieve the tasks set out for them? Then, all he had to do was read the first question, close his eyes and envision each student and write a reply. He was amazed at how every student had a completely different comment.

Going forward from this point on, always write in response to a question. (I will explain in more detail on the following pages.)

How the development of a house can help you write your book and banish writer's block.

If I had a penny for every time someone said to me they couldn't write because they have writer's block, I'd be very rich. The only reason writers suffer from writer's block is because they didn't plan it properly. Think of it this way, when you build a house, you don't just bring your tools to the site, and hope that it'll get built. You need to plan it carefully, get an architect to draw up the plans, order in the materials and so on. The same goes for writing.

It's vitally important to have an outline of your book. Just as an architect's plans will show the building manager exactly what the house should look like when it's built, the outline will tell the writer the whole book from start to finish before a single word is written. And if you know what your book is going to be about, chapter-by-chapter, you'll know exactly what to say and writer's block will be nonexistent. I'll tell you more about this later in the chapter, and proceeding chapters.

Now I can literally hear the screams of despair from the few "free-flow" writers reading this. Now some people have the natural ability to just sit down and write without a plan. If you are one of those people, I applaud you; you're definitely more creative than me.

However, in most cases for fiction writers, you get lost in the plot and have to keep on paging back, to make sure the story flows smoothly and there isn't any continuity errors. As for non-fiction, many free flow writers have to page back to make sure they haven't repeated information or missed anything out. By having a plan (outline), this eliminates that whole process and just makes it a hell of a lot easier to write your masterpiece.

The Winning Writing Machine Technique.

This is one of the most powerful strategies I'm going to show you. Forget everything you have been taught, clear your mind and make way for his revolutionary technique. When one of my mentors taught me this technique, I thought it was lunacy. But I implemented it, and now it's part of my everyday writing technique.

So strap yourself in, the rides about to start.

Three words are all the human brain needs to create a complete story.

Understand this concept and you'll have the essence of speedwriting at your fingertips.

The three words vary, but there's always a similarity. They are meaningful and have more meaning than simply their definition. They have a connotation as well as a definition.

To most people, these words are simply nouns and verbs, but to a prolific writer, they are the key to speedwriting.

Let me give you a brief example: If I gave you the words **"dark, banana, corner"**, your mind, will instantly and clearly develop some sort of a story. It could be a man eating a banana, standing on the corner of the road in the darkness. Or someone slips on a banana peel, hitting their knee on the corner of a table because they couldn't see it in the dark. Or someone looks at the corners of the banana going dark as it starts to rot. The possibilities are endless. If I was in the room of 50 people and gave them the same three words, all the stories will be different in their own minds. The important thing to remember is, they all will have some sort of story. All of them wouldn't complain that the three words couldn't bring up an image or story in their mind. In fact I bet you have a little story in your mind right now?

The amazing thing is, your brain will do it over and over again to different words. Now it's important to forget about using boring words like "I, the, a, or it", they have to be dynamic for the technique to work properly.

If you ever have a problem with this technique, do as I would do. Get out your dictionary, open it to a random page and the first verb or noun you see, jot it down, and then choose another from a different page and one more from a different page. Now you have three dynamic words you can use to create a story.

If you follow the instructions of the upcoming writing exercise, you'll be producing stories at a phenomenal rate.

The simple five minute exercise that will have your creative juices flowing.

Remember when I mentioned in the previous chapter, that when we write to deadlines, we write quickly. And when we write quickly, we write the way we talk. Well, I'm now going to show you a very simple, yet effective technique of writing to five minute deadlines.

What you are about to discover in the next few paragraphs will change your writing career forever, you'll never suffer from writer's block and procrastination will just be another word.

You're about to take part in an exciting writing exercise that only takes five minutes. All I ask is that you take it seriously and obey the rules I'm about to set out. If you do these two things, I promise you, you'll instantly know you'll be able to write your book in the fastest time possible and your life will be changed forever.

Just because this is an "exercise," it doesn't mean you can skip this part, nor have a break. This is the crux of the whole writing process. If you skip this exercise, you'll be throwing the money you spent on this away. Trust me, its well worth the five minutes, as you will soon see.

Five rules that will enable you to write your book in under a month.

For this exercise you'll need a count-down timer, I find my mobile phone works a treat for this, most phones have this option now. You'll also need a pen and lined paper, or if you prefer, a computer or laptop.

You're now going to do some writing. But before you do, I want you to read the instructions very carefully. I've tried to make it as simple as possible. Read them until you understand exactly what you're required to do before attempting the exercise.

Next, **obey all the rules set out,** if you don't, you won't benefit from this exercise and get the results you're looking for.

The **first rule** is, set your timer for five minutes. This is all you'll need, remember, five minutes only, no more, no less.

Second rule; write as fast as you possibly can for those five minutes, when the timer sounds, finish. The faster you writer, the better your writing will be.

Rule number three: *Do not think*. This may be hard for you to grasp, but I'll explain.

Whatever comes to the forefront of your mind that's what you'll write down. ***Do not edit*** during the five minutes, if you make a mistake, it can be rectified later. You're writing a story not a bunch of disjointed words, but don't let your mind get in the way. Just write down whatever comes into your head. Remember the faster you write, the better it will be.

Start with the magic number.

In a second, I'm going to give you three words. This brings me to **rule number four**. Use one of your three words to kick off your writing. So, if I gave you the words "disaster, endless and shift", you would start with one of those three. You ***can't*** start with: Once upon a time..., A long time ago..., It was a cold and dark September..., cut that rubbish out. It's essential you start with one of those three words. If you decide to start with any of the above

I've mentioned, be warned, I have your details, I'll hunt you down and fan you with a brick end. (Only joking, bricks are too messy.)

Now you can add the letter "s" to the end, or even the letters "ing" or "ly", that's perfectly fine, in fact you can add any suffix you want to, just make sure you start with one of those three words.

Finally, **rule number five.** The other two words ***must*** appear in the ***first*** paragraph. Always remember, the faster you write the better it will be.

As soon as you see the three words, choose one to start with, start your timer, and begin writing immediately. Whatever you do, don't sit there and ponder on what you want to say. **Don't think, just write.** If you start to think, you won't get the benefit of the exercise and you'll just end up messing things up!

Here are some words: **Red, car, happy, Father, bridge, beautiful, transport, oppressed, bed.**

Now, pick every third word to get your three words and start writing as fast as you can. GO! GO! GO!

Read this only after you have finished the exercise!

Now, if you did finish the exercise, and I really hope you did, you're probably very impressed with yourself. Most people write about two thirds of the page. If you didn't, go back and try the exercise again with three different words and you'll soon see two thirds really isn't that difficult.

Now for something quite shocking! If you want to write your book in under a month, whether it's fiction or non-fiction, and you wrote on average two thirds of a page in five minutes, you'll have to *slow right down!* At that rate, you could produce a non-fiction book in 25 hours and a 400 page (super novel), in just 50 hours of writing.

Now for the really exciting part! Read what you've just written. Go on, I'll still be here when you've finished...

Done? I bet it's good, isn't it? If fact, it might just be the best thing you've ever written.

Every time I ask a writing class to do this simple exercise, I pick one at random and ask them to read it out. Every time, they are astonished at the quality of their work, so much so, that all the other members of the group are afraid to read out theirs, as they don't think it's good enough, yet each one has produced work of high quality.

The fundamentals behind this technique, and why it works so well!

Let me break this process down, and analyse the components. Soon you'll see why this technique is so powerful and the benefits you'll have if you copy this technique.

For a start, this is the very core of speedwriting. Then, you need to realise you were writing for five minutes solid, not hesitating and writer's block didn't even come in the equation. Now you may have suffered from writers block before, but with this exercise, (if done properly,) it's a thing of the past. If you did suffer from writer's block, then you were thinking what to say, and that's cheating.

Next, your writing was "off the cuff", there wasn't any prior planning of what you wanted to say, so there wasn't a few pages of "fluff" until you got your point across.

Your story started as soon as you started typing or writing, and it was interesting right off the bat.

The reason it all went so incredibly well is because you started with a power word, and not a dull or boring word like "the". I find that if you start with "the", it takes you a while to get your point across and let me tell you, your ideal reader doesn't want to read 10 pages of rubbish before they get to the good bits. Do you? No I thought not. All they would do is put your book down and find another that satisfies their needs.

They want action from the very first word, that's what sells, if you can grab your reader and immediately throw then into the situation you've created, then you're in a much better position of seeing your book on both the brick and mortar, and digital bookshop shelves.

Another advantage of this writing technique is that you had very clear instructions to follow. Write as fast as you can for five minutes without thinking. Start with one of the three power words given and the other two must be in the first paragraph. The faster you write, the better it will be. You were writing a story and not a load of disjointed thoughts.

When you have these clear instructions, you will never – and I mean never, suffer from writer's block. If you simply free your mind to write on autopilot, there's nothing that can block it.

Next, you were given a five-minute deadline to write to, after that time was up, you had to stop. As I've mentioned before, the closer we get to a deadline, the more productive we become. You don't believe me? Invite the in-laws for dinner tonight. As the time for them to arrive gets nearer, watch how fast you clean the house.

Lastly, one of the greatest benefits of this exercise is that you realise writing is really fun and enjoyable. It's not tedious or laborious as most people think. It's just plain great fun.

One final warning about this strategy!

I'm going to have a little chat to you about human psychology, something I learned in my brief studies as a criminal psychologist. People believe that there is a direct link between the length of time it takes someone to produce, or do something, and its worth. We have been brought up to think that the longer someone spends creating something, the better quality it will be. I've just proven to you that this isn't the case. However, if you tell someone you wrote your book in under a month, they'll instinctively think, that it's of little or no value to them. So with this in mind, I ask you to please keep this strategy between fellow writers and not share it with the public, for your own benefit.

So if people ask you how long it took to write your book, tell them many years. And when your next one comes out the next month, tell them you were working on that for years too.

Questions normally related to this chapter.

When I conduct my writing classes, and I have just gone through this exercise with my students, I invariably get ask the same questions over and over. So I'm going to take the opportunity here to answer some of them. If you have any more after you've finished reading this, then please feel free to email me at **questions@simplewritingstrategies.com.** Remember, I'll be dealing with the support, no one else.

How many words can you get on a page?

The answer is around 350 words per page, now this doesn't matter if you write it out manually or type it up on a computer, it still adds up to 350. Even on a published book, you will get around 350 words to a page.

How many pages should there be in a chapter?

There is no real definitive answer to this question as it varies from author to author. However, in saying that, I believe the perfect amount of pages should be around ten pages per chapter.

Here's why...

Firstly, you can say a lot in ten pages, it's more than enough to say what you have to. More to the point, by keeping it ten pages, you force yourself to get your point across sooner, making it more punchy and sharp. It also allows you to get rid of any fluff.

Another very good reason for making it ten pages is it's a great benefit to your reader. Again, let me explain. The modern person works 40 or more hours a week, making it hard to get any reading done. When they do get a chance, it's during their coffee or lunch break, or when they're on the bus on the way to work. The last thing the reader wants is to start a chapter and not finish it. I'm the same. I have to finish a chapter before putting it down. So a ten-page chapter fits quite nicely into a person's daily routine.

Think of it this way, if they read a chapter every time they open your book, they'll finish it sooner. This has a great benefit to you, because the sooner they finish it, the sooner they'll be out to buy your second book.

A little later I will show you a technique that will get you pumping out ten page chapters time after time.

How many chapters should I have?

The answer really depends on what genre you are writing to. Not many people know that each genre has an average page count. This is based on what the readers are used to.

Also, this is something you need to be aware of – if you find yourself trying to get it published traditionally, publishers tend to print certain genres around an average amount of pages because they are aware of what number sells best.

So what are the mystical averages that make a book so marketable?

I've broken it down to the average pages and chapters. It would be in your interest to remember these for future reference. These are not set in stone, so don't think you have to stick to them religiously. I've seen books break these rules time and time again, however,

keep in mind publishers have done extensive research to find the optimal amount of pages, so it's worth heeding.

Genre	Average Pages	Average Chapters
Super Novel	400	40

Romance	350	35
Fantasy	350	35
Horror	350	35
Science Fiction	300	30
Crime / Thriller	280	28
Action / Adventure	280	28
Western	200	20
Teen Novel	200	20
How to	200	20
Age 7 - 12	150	15
Movie Script	120	12
Children's	100	10

There isn't an average for autobiographies and biographies for the simple reason that each person is different. The more active a person is, the more stories they have, and the more pages it will be.

I'm assuming you already have a great idea for a book, whether it's fiction or non-fiction. You probably know what twists and turns you're going to provide or any other information you want to share. If you don't, don't worry all will be revealed in a later chapter. You may even have an ideal number of chapters you will like to write. All I say is try stick to the guidelines above. They've been set out for a reason. I've had students attending my workshops that have paid dearly because a publisher won't accept their book because they didn't adhere to the guidelines.

I sincerely hope you're enjoying reading this book and starting to see the power of writing with these techniques.

In the next chapter we're going even deeper, and I'm going to show you how to write an outline so you'll know what's going to be on every page of your book before you even write it. See you on the other side...

Chapter 6

The Master Blueprint! Knowing what's on every page before you even start writing.

Having a blueprint of your book prepared is one of the most important things you can do before you start. If you know exactly what is going to happen in your book, chapter by chapter, you'll find it incredibly easy to write. You won't suffer from writer's block, (I have already proven that), but you'll also write your book in record time.

Okay disclaimer time.

I'm not going to sit here and say to you that having a blueprint is the only writing technique on the planet that works. There are other techniques out there that work considerably well for other writers. All I'm saying is that I have tried some of these techniques and they just didn't work for me. The blueprint techniques I'm about to show you are, in my opinion, the best and the quickest I have come across.

Yes, you may have heard authors say that they just sat down in front of the computer and started to type until the book was finished. I'm not stating that it can't be done, in fact I know of a few writers that prefer this method because they can write without interrupting their flow, but I also know many had to do a lot of re-writes due to continuity errors and the like.

Then there are those that say that they didn't write it, the characters did. They were just the tools in which the characters used to tell their tale. I can certainly see their point of view; you can most definitely, get swept away with a character. However, the fact of the matter is, you have to do the writing yourself, no one else will do it for you. Hold on – wait a moment, I should really say "in most cases". There are a few cases where the author has got others to write his book for him and cashed in on it. However, in most cases, you'll have to write it.

Have one interesting point to say in each chapter.

I know of a few writers that join my workshops that say they don't really have anything interesting to say for each chapter.

That may be the case, and it's not the be all and end all. However, you want your book to be riveting enough so that readers just can't put it down, and leaves them begging for more after they've finished it. So it's in your interest to add at least one interesting point to each chapter. For you non-fiction writers, offer part of a solution in every chapter, so that it keeps them page turning. You owe it to your readers.

Why it's important to have a blueprint before you start.

In my professional opinion, I'm convinced that for your book to be a raging success, and to make it really easy for you to write your book, you need a blueprint on the entire book from start to finish. You need to know what's going to happen on every page of the book, know what plot developments will unfold, what information the reader needs to know, what message you want to convey and the order of your chapters. Now before you go off on one and start yelling "You're suffocating my creativity!" Know that that's far from the truth. All I'm trying to do is eliminate any obstacles you may face along the way.

So with that said, let's begin...

It starts with an outline.

An outline is no doubt instrumental to the success of your book. It's the place where we have to start, but don't worry, I have a technique that gets it finished fairly quickly.

One of the important reasons, if not the most important reason we have an outline, is to ensure you follow the publisher's guidelines. Even if you want to self-publish, the printer will require certain guidelines to be met before they decide to print your book.

You also want to make sure you include all the information you want to include in your book. The last thing you want is to finish the book, only to realise you have missed out an important part and you have to re-write it.

The objective of the outline is to show you exactly what you're going to cover and in which chapter. It'll also save you months of hard work. You won't have to wonder what the next twist in the plot will be, or what you want to write about, it'll be all there, nicely bundled in the outline.

The Chapter Outline.

Now I know you're chomping at the bit to get started, that's good, keep that enthusiasm. But before we start, as mentioned above, you need a chapter outline. As I go through the process with you, realise that you have to do this **for every chapter**, like a sort of "rinse and repeat" process.

Right, let's begin...

For this you'll need a scrapbook or a computer, I personally use a scrapbook for the process so I'm not flicking between screens.

Okay, here we go. Down the side of your page, list the numbers 1 down to 18.

Now next to each number, jot down a sentence that will convey what you want to talk about in the chapter. This could be an idea, a concept, a piece of dialogue or a plot development. Do this for all 18 lines. By doing this, you have just created 18 things you want to chat about or let your reader know in each chapter.

If you've more than 18 things you want to talk about, just jot down 18. You can take the excess ideas and put them into another chapter.

Let's make this fun shall we? Why not get your pen and paper out right now and jot down the 18 points for the very first chapter of your book. Go on, I'll be here ready to continue when you get back.

If you can't think of 18, don't worry it's a problem a lot of people face. Luckily I have a solution for that and it's called…

The journalists six W's.

The 6 W's are words which are: **Who, What, When, Where, Why and How.**

So, let's say you have only managed 12 things you want to put in your chapter, you're short 6. All you need to do is ask yourself one "who" question, one "what" question, one "when" question, one "where" question, one "why" question and one "how" question. If you only have 10 things and you need another 8, just ask a variation of the above.

Let me give you an example of what I'm trying to say.

Let's say you're writing a story called Goldilocks and the three bears. (I'm using this as an example because almost everyone knows this story.)

Let's say for arguments sake, you have 12 ideas for chapter 4, when goldilocks enters the house and sees the porridge. You're missing 6. Ask yourself these questions.

1.) Who left the porridge on the table?

2.) What's the first thing Goldilocks does as she enters the house?

3.) When does Goldilocks decide to eat the porridge?

4.) Where are the occupants of the house?

5.) Why have they left the porridge on the table?

6.) How do the bears react to the stolen porridge?

You see, it's pretty easy when you ask yourself the 6 W's. If you're ever stuck on what to put down for the 18 things in your chapter, just think of the 6 W's.

Have you got them jotted down yet? You have! Excellent, we shall continue then.

So now you have the 18 ideas you want in your chapter, that's fantastic. What I'm going to tell you now will probably make you a bit angry but it's done for a reason.

Look carefully at the 18 ideas. Now find 3 that you think are the least interesting of the 18. These will be the three that you think won't benefit the reader or the ones you struggled with and just put in there because you needed 18.

Take the 3 and remove them from the 18 you had for the chapter. I told you, you'll be mad, after all you've just spent your time trying to come up with 18 and now I'm telling you to subtract three. By doing this you're writing will be much tighter.

So now you angrily crossed out three and you now have 15 ideas you would like in your chapter. A little later on I'll explain why this is important, but for now, we continue with the process.

The spice that makes it all work!

Now we have come to the most important part in the whole process. If your book doesn't read well or you have trouble writing it, it's because you haven't paid attention and implemented this process properly.

Here's what you do next...

Take the 15 elements of the chapter and arrange them in the best order for your reader. This can be in chronological order, smallest to biggest, most important to least important or whatever order you feel would benefit the reader. Take a step back and put yourself into the shoes of your reader. Try and see what they would want to read and the order the points need to go in.

The biggest problem is that writers think they have already put the ideas in order. It's always wise to go though them a couple of times, just to make sure.

The proof in the pudding (or porridge) is in the eating.

Maybe you've grasped what I'm trying to teach straight off the bat, maybe you're struggling to see what it is I want from you. To make it super easy for you, I'm going to show you exactly what I mean. Not only that I'm going to give you examples of fiction and non-fiction.

So let's start with fiction. Using Goldilocks and the three bears, I'll show you how we get the outline for, let's say for arguments sake, chapter 4.

First, I've got the 18 ideas I want to tell the reader.

1.) Description of the outside of bear's house.
2.) Who left the porridge on the table?
3.) How did Goldilocks get to the house?
4.) Goldilocks feelings about entering the house.
5.) Description of the inside of the house.
6.) How do the bears react to the stolen porridge?
7.) Goldilocks' reaction to the first bowl of porridge.
8.) When does Goldilocks decide to eat the porridge?
9.) Goldilocks' reaction to the second bowl of porridge.
10.) Where are the occupants of the house?
11.) Goldilocks' reaction to the third bowl of porridge.

12.) Goldilocks gets sleepy after eating the small bowl.

13.) What's the first thing Goldilocks does as she enters the house?

14.) Why have the bears left the porridge on the table?

15.) Goldilocks finds the beds.

16.) Why can't she sleep in the big bed?

17.) What do the bears do to Goldilocks when they find her?

18.) Whose bed does Goldilocks finally sleep in?

Okay, there you have it, 18 ideas I want in this chapter, let's not waste any time, I'll cut three I don't need. You may decide to cut a different three, that's fine, we each have a different thought process. Please note that there are no right or wrong answers.

1.) Description of the outside of bear's house.

2.) Who left the porridge on the table?

3.) How did Goldilocks get to the house?

4.) Goldilocks feelings about entering the house.

5.) Description of the inside of the house.

6.) How do the bears react to the stolen porridge?

7.) When does Goldilocks decide to eat the porridge?

8.) Where are the occupants of the house?

9.) Goldilocks gets sleepy after eating the small bowl.

10.) What's the first thing Goldilocks does as she enters the house?

11.) Why have the bears left the porridge on the table?

12.) Goldilocks finds the beds.

13.) Why can't she sleep in the big bed?

14.) What do the bears do to Goldilocks when they find her?

15.) Whose bed does Goldilocks finally sleep in?

Now they all look a bit jumbled in that order, time to put them in the order I want them on the book.

1.) Description of the outside of bear's house.

2.) Where are the occupants of the house?

3.) How did Goldilocks get to the house?

4.) Description of the inside of the house.

5.) Goldilocks feelings about entering the house.

6.) What's the first thing Goldilocks does as she enters the house?

7.) Who left the porridge on the table?

8.) When does Goldilocks decide to eat the porridge?

9.) Why have the bears left the porridge on the table?

10.) Goldilocks gets sleepy after eating the small bowl.

11.) Goldilocks finds the beds.

12.) Why can't she sleep in the big bed?

13.) Whose bed does Goldilocks finally sleep in?

14.) How do the bears react to the stolen porridge?

15.) What do the bears do to Goldilocks when they find her?

That has taken me just a few minutes to do the outline of this chapter. It should take you roughly the same amount of time.

Now for the non-fiction example, I'm going to show you the outline I did for this very chapter you are reading now. I know, it's a bit lazy because I'm copying what I've already done, but by doing so, it'll give you a really clear indication of how works, as you're reading the finished product right now.

1.) Importance of a blueprint.

2.) Conclusion

3.) The 6 W's

4.) An interesting point for each chapter.

5.) The 18 points or ideas strategy.

6.) Introduce Chapter outline.

7.) Importance of an outline.

8.) Why the 15 points are so important to chapter development.

9.) Use Goldilocks an example.

10.) Subtraction of 3.

11.) Fiction example of 18.

12.) Fiction example of subtracting 3.

13.) Fiction example of changing the order.

14.) Non-fiction example of 18.

15.) Non-fiction example of subtracting 3.

16.) Non-fiction example for changing the order.

17.) Explain the idea of swapping the points around.

18.) Introduction to the chapter.

So there's the 18 points I originally had when I drew up the outline for this chapter. Now I'm going to do the same thing as I did with the fiction. I'm going to take away three to leave me with 15. Again, if you were writing this chapter, you might decide to eliminate a different three.

So here goes...

1.) Importance of a blueprint.
2.) Conclusion
3.) The 6 W's
4.) An interesting point for each chapter.
5.) Introduce Chapter outline.
6.) Importance of an outline.
7.) Subtraction of 3.
8.) Fiction example of 18.
9.) Fiction example of subtracting 3.
10.) Fiction example of changing the order.
11.) Non-fiction example of 18.
12.) Non-fiction example of subtracting 3.
13.) Non-fiction example for changing the order.
14.) Explain the idea of swapping the points around.
15.) Introduction to the chapter.

So now I've got my selection of 15, this is what went into the chapter you're reading. Time to put them in the best order for you, my lovely reader...

1.) Introduction to the chapter.
2.) An interesting point for each chapter.
3.) Importance of a blueprint.
4.) Importance of an outline.
5.) Introduce Chapter outline.
6.) The 6 W's
7.) Subtraction of 3.
8.) Explain the idea of swapping the points around.
9.) Fiction example of 18.
10.) Fiction example of subtracting 3.
11.) Fiction example of changing the order.
12.) Non-fiction example of 18.
13.) Non-fiction example of subtracting 3.

14.) Non-fiction example for changing the order.
15.) Conclusion

And there you have it folks, a chapter outline for both fiction and non-fiction. Originally I was going to do another non-fiction example, but I decided it would be beneficial for you to see it in action, and to be honest a little fun for me too.

Guess what? By following the instructions, you now you've a pretty good idea about what you're going to write in your first chapter, no stone is left unturned, it's as clear as day. How exciting is that?

All you have to do now is do exactly the same for every chapter in your book. Remember, stick to the guidelines shown previously. Ignore them at your peril. When you've finished all the outline chapters, you'll have a complete book outline, and a sense of real accomplishment. It's like laying the foundations to a building, building the walls and putting on the roof. Now all you have to do is pad it out.

So how long does an outline take you? To be quite honest, it doesn't really matter; it's down to you. Obviously the faster the better, but even if you take a little longer than expected, you'll still be way ahead of the pack. While other writer's are dithering, thinking of what to put in their book, you know exactly what you want to write about.

In the next chapter we're going to swiftly move down the writing production line, from outline to blueprint!

Chapter 7

Continuing with the Master Blueprint! Moving along the Writing Production Line.

Okay let's recap a little bit here. So far you've been shown that to write well, you need to write the way you talk. If you write the way you talk, you'll write quickly. If you write quickly, you'll be a prolific writer. You now also know how to choose a topic that'll keep your reader coming back for more, by writing a book that the reader wants and needs.

I've also proven to you that anyone can write using the exercise I provided in chapter 5, where you wrote to a five-minute deadline, using 3 power words, with the instructions that you use one of the power words to start the sentence, and the other two in the first paragraph.

In the last chapter we spoke about the importance of having a blueprint, and the first part was to create an outline for every chapter in the book, so you would know exactly what to write before you even started.

Hopefully by now, you should have an outline for your book. In each chapter you should've chosen 18 points or ideas you would like to tell the reader. You then should've deleted the least three important, leaving you with 15. After that you should've re-arranged the 15 in an order that would suit you and the reader. Now you should have a complete outline for each chapter of your book. All of this should've taken you several hours to complete. If you haven't done it yet, why not? Why don't you change the scenery a little and take a little break from this book. Go complete your outline now; I'll still be here when you get back. If you want to read the whole book first to gain an understanding of what's needed of you, don't worry; I won't hold it against you, I just thought you were eager to get your book written, that's all.

Now you may be itching to get your book done, but as I said, by doing the outline, you're already way ahead of the pack.

Now on to the next step...

Chugging along the Blueprint Creation Process!

Okay, like the Outline, I'm going to show you how to formulate a blueprint for just one chapter, all you have to do is repeat the process for the rest of the chapters.

I'm going to go on the basis that you have taken my words of advise and already done the chapter outline.

So, start by picking any chapter outline you've created and have a look at what you've written. Now go to each of the 15 items of information and ask yourself why that item is significant. Then write a significant sentence about each item.

Right, let me explain in more detail by giving you an example. Again, I'll be using Goldilocks and the 3 bears as an example, but you'll see they easily work for both. Now it may seem basic, however, I've done this for a reason because I want you to understand the technique that's involved. Once you have a full understanding of this technique, you could write any book your heart's desire.

Let's take a look at Goldilocks and the three bear's example.

Here's the chapter outline as we discussed in the previous chapter.

1.) Description of the outside of bear's house.

2.) Where are the occupants of the house?

3.) How did Goldilocks get to the house?

4.) Description of the inside of the house.

5.) Goldilocks feelings about entering the house.

6.) What's the first thing Goldilocks does as she enters the house?

7.) Who left the porridge on the table?

8.) When does Goldilocks decide to eat the porridge?

9.) Why have the bears left the porridge on the table?

10.) Goldilocks gets sleepy after eating the small bowl.

11.) Goldilocks finds the beds.

12.) Why can't she sleep in the big bed?

13.) Whose bed does Goldilocks finally sleep in?

14.) How do the bears react to the stolen porridge?

15.) What do the bears do to Goldilocks when they find her?

Now let's make a significant sentence for each one.

1.) The description of the outside of the bear's house is essential to the story development.

2.) The occupants have gone for a walk in the forest.

3.) Goldilocks sees no one is home through the window and opens the door and steps inside.

4.) The description of the inside of the house tells us who lives there.

5.) Goldilocks is a bit apprehensive as she enters the house.

6.) Goldilocks looks around the house to make sure no one is there.

7.) It seems the bear's left the porridge on the table.

8.) Now that no one is in the house Goldilocks decides to eat the porridge before it goes cold.

9.) The porridge was left on the table because it was too hot.

10.) Now that she's eaten her fill, Goldilocks is tired and finds a bed to sleep on.

11.) Goldilocks finds the beds.

12.) As Goldilocks tries the big bed, she finds it too hard to sleep on.

13.) Goldilocks then tries the small bed and finds it perfect for her.

14.) The mama and papa bear are angry and baby bear cries because his porridge has been eaten.

15.) Goldilocks is woken by the bear's that chase her out the house.

That's the next step finished. All you're doing is changing the idea or important element into a significant statement. The next part in the blueprint production line is simple. All I want you to do is turn the statement into a question.

Now I know some of you may have already changed your ideas into a statement, only to revert it back to a question again. There is an important reason for doing this. Firstly it opens your mind to the process, subconsciously giving you ideas on what to write about, making it easier to write your book when the time comes, and it also has to do with the way our brains function. As I've mentioned before, it's far easier to respond to a question than it is to respond to a statement.

Moving forward, I'm now going to change each statement to a question. If you're following me during this process, please leave three spaces between each question. All will be revealed as you read on, but for now, just leave three spaces.

1.) Why is the description to the bear's house important to the story?

2.) Where have the occupants gone for a walk?

3.) What does Goldilocks do as she approaches the house?

4.) What does the description of the inside of the house tell the reader?

5.) How does Goldilocks feel as she enters the house?

6.) What does Goldilocks do as she enters the house?

7.) What does Goldilocks see sitting on the table?

8.) What does Goldilocks decide to do with the porridge?

9.) What's the reason for the porridge being there in the first place?

10.) After eating the porridge, how does Goldilocks feel?

11.) What does Goldilocks find in the bedroom?

12.) Why does Goldilocks find the big bed uncomfortable?

13.) How does Goldilocks feel about the small bed?

14.) How to the bears react to the missing porridge?

15.) What do they do to Goldilocks after they find her sleeping in their bed?

Okay, so far so good. This isn't that hard is it? On to the next step!

Why the three blank lines?

Hopefully, you have left the three lines I asked you to. If you haven't, go back and re-write them leaving the three blank lines, or if you're using a computer, just go to each question and create three spaces. You're now going to find out why I asked you to do this.

Remember the exercise with the three power words? Well, you will be entering three power words for each question. (I can just imagine the light bulb above your head flickering on.) This is the part of the process where it comes together for most people. If it hasn't yet, it soon will, just keep reading.

Go to the first question, read it and close your eyes and let your imagination paint you a picture. You should have quite a clear picture in your mind. Now think of three words to describe that sentence. It could be any three words you can think of. It could be a sight, sound smell, texture, flavour, colour, emotion, a piece of furniture or even an animal. The possibilities are endless. Just make sure it's not a, the, it, or and. It needs to be power words.

Once you have the words in your mind, enter them onto the paper or on the screen, just below the question. Do this for all 15 questions.

So let's revisit Goldilocks again.

1.) Why is the description to the bear's house important to the story?
   A.) Approaching
   B.) Windows
   C.) Straw.

2.) Where have the occupants gone for a walk?
   A.) Forest
   B.) Door
   C.) Hot

3.) What does Goldilocks do as she approaches the house?
   A.) Peering
   B.) Tiptoe
   C.) Empty

4.) What does the description of the inside of the house tell the reader?
   A.) Sweet
   B.) Portrait
   C.) Stepping

5.) How does Goldilocks feel as she enters the house?

A.) Scared
B.) Reluctant
C.) Heartbeat

6.) What does Goldilocks do as she enters the house?
A.) Looking
B.) Search

C.) Relieved

7.) What does Goldilocks see sitting on the table?
A.) Surprised
B.) Steaming
C.) Aroma

8.) What does Goldilocks decide to do with the porridge?
A.) Shame
B.) Gobble
C.) Certain
9.) What's the reason for the porridge being there in the first place?
A.) Scorched
B.) Tongue
C.) Immediate.

10.) After eating the porridge, how does Goldilocks feel?
A.) Wolfing
B.) Tired
C.) Yawning

11.) What does Goldilocks find in the bedroom?
A.) Stumble
B.) Three
C.) Beds

12.) Why does Goldilocks find the big bed uncomfortable?
A.) Jumps
B.) Uncomfortable
C.) Hard

13.) How does Goldilocks feel about the small bed?
A.) Nice
B.) Sinks
C.) Hopping

14.) How to the bears react to the missing porridge?
A.) Opening
B.) Shocked

C.) Crying

15.) What do they do to Goldilocks after they find her sleeping in their bed?
A.) Suddenly
B.) Snoring
C.) Roar

There you have it, the three power words for each question. Yes, I know, you came up with something different, that's good, everyone is different, and that's what makes us so unique.

Now all you have to do is "Rinse and Repeat" for every chapter. Turn each idea into a statement, then each statement into a question and then think of three power words for each question. On a side note, if you have already got a question for the idea as you went through the 6 W's, then I suppose it's alright to leave it as it is, no one is going to shout at you for doing that.

Once you have done it for each chapter, guess what? You have finished your book blueprint. Depending on how fast you go through the chapters, this could be done in a day or two, perhaps even less than that.

Now you are ready to Start Your Book.

Another quick recap…

We're almost at the process of actually starting to write your book. I know it took a while to get here, but I'm sure you'll agree it was worth it.

So let's just recap how we turn out outline into a blueprint.

Pick any chapter outline. (I would recommend starting at chapter 1, but it's your choice.)

Write a significant sentence about each point.
Change the significant statement into a question.
Leave three spaces between each question.
Write three power words below each question.
Do this for all chapters until blueprint is complete.

Writing your first chapter

Right, now I want you to go to any chapter in your blueprint and pick any question. Personally, I would work from chapter 1 and work chronologically from 1 to 15, but it's not necessary.

Now get yourself a timer of some sort. As I mentioned before most mobile phones now have a countdown timer, if you have one, use that. I find this to work the best.

On a side note, don't get a kitchen timer; the ticking will only distract you.

Now you've got the timer, you've set it for 5 minutes. You've picked your chapter and question you would like to start with. Set the timer and go! Remember to start with a power word and use the other two in the first paragraph. Write as fast as you can. Don't think about what you're writing and **DON'T** edit as you go along. The faster you write, the better you write.

As soon as the timer stops, you must stop. Find another question and do it all over again. If you do it chronologically, as soon as you've finished question number 15, you've written your first chapter. I bet that feels fantastic, doesn't it?

Techniques for writing a "transition" between points

If it's non-fiction, it should read quite well, because all you're doing is listing information, listing information, listing information. With fiction however, this could be tricky, as after each question it may it may not flow smoothly in places. The way we remedy this scenario is by having a smooth transition between the two questions.

Let me explain a little better. Let's say, for arguments sake, the third item was about a speedboat, the forth item was about a house. So you read about the speedboat and then about the house, but it just doesn't make enough sense at this point in time. You need to bring your reader from the speedboat to the house smoothly. So what's the one word that connects the speedboat to the house? This connecting word can be anything you choose, depending on your story. For this example, let's use the word "chasing". Now set the timer for one minute, no more. When the timer starts, write a one or two sentence paragraph that joins the two ideas. And just in case you were wondering, you don't have to start with the power word.

"Simon pulled the throttle down harder as the speedboat hit the bank of the river, throwing it through the air. It came down with a mighty thud as the engine cut out. He turned to see the men still chasing him as he ran up to the house, frantically looking for the right key for the front door."

This won't always happen; you'll find, as you get better at writing, the transitions will appear naturally.

Why only five minutes?

From experience, your mind will initially give you the really good stuff, after about 5 minutes it starts to give you fluff and padding. Now if you carry on and start writing drivel, an editor will just eliminate it anyway. So to save time and the editor's sanity, keep it to five minutes.

The reason behind the 15 questions!

Remember when you did the exercise I said I'll explain why you needs 15 points of interest? Well here's the explanation and I'm sure you'll all be saying "Ahh – that's why" at the end.

Now I was never good at math, but I'm sure I can explain these simple equations to you. Remember I said to you that if you write for a solid five minutes, you should get down about two-thirds of a page? I also said that the perfect amount of pages in a chapter is around ten, this is what publishers prefer. Well if you take two-thirds of a page times fifteen questions, you get – ta da – ten pages of writing.

Working on that premise, you'll be producing a ten-page chapter in about 75 minutes of writing. Now do you see how fast you can write your book?

But what if I have more to say?

This will be by far, the biggest problem you'll face when writing your book, actually physically stopping yourself after the five minutes is up.

Look, I'm not going to be there watching over your shoulder, so if you feel you have some more to add, maybe more description, I can't stop you. But if it were me writing the book, I'd stop at five minutes. Besides, you want the book finished in the shortest time possible right? So why make more work for yourself and take longer to do it?

Can't I just write a blueprint for one chapter and then write it?

NO WAY! You need to write the blueprint for the entire book otherwise how do you know if you haven't repeated information in a previous chapter. The whole idea for the blueprint is you know exactly what's going to be in your book before you write it. It's so much easier to see an entire overview of the whole book in blueprint form, rather that flicking back to see if you've already written the information. Also looking at the whole blueprint will just spur you on to get the book written.

This takes all the hard work out of writing, you know what you're going to say, you just sit down and write it. You don't have to flip though pages to refresh your memory, you're blueprint is your memory.

One great thing about a blueprint is, that if you take a break for a few months (personally, unless you become unwell or there are problems in your family life, there should be a reason why you should take a break,) however, for whatever reason you have to take a break for an extended period, when you go back to your blueprint, you can pick up exactly where you left off. As soon as you read the question and the three power words, the scenario you visualised months ago, springs back in to your mind's eye.

Captivating from the first word

I'm going to mention the importance of grabbing your reader from the start again, because I feel this is vitally important to the success of your book.

The first person you must impress is the editor or agent. Let me tell you these chaps are tough cookies. They get anywhere between 10 to 300 proposals a day, possibly more. The only way to separate yours from the others is to write an irresistible lead. Something so powerful, it picks the editor or agent off their chairs and slams them into the story with so much force, they can't put the manuscript down. I can't stress enough how important this element is to your success.

There might be several exciting elements to your book, pick the most exciting one and start from there.

Once you have the most exciting element, I want you to close your eyes and imagine the scene – visualise the whole process. See the scene that your reader will see, the scene you **want** the reader to see.

So what are the three words that best describe that scene? Jot them down. Set your timer for five minutes. Start with one of the three words, the other two must appear in the first paragraph. Write as fast as you can. Don't think, don't edit. The faster you write the better your writing will be.

When you finish, you'll have a lead that will grab any agent or editor.

Ending with style.

It really doesn't matter how you end the book, you're certainly not going to get rejected for a poor ending. However, I always try and inspire my workshop students to write a good ending. Here's how you do it. Every book in the world has a topic, and can usually be summed up in one word. Each book is different, so the summation word will obviously be different. However, if I had to ask you to surmise your book in one word, you would probably be able to do it.

So with this in mind, if you're writing on paper, take out a ·blank piece and at the bottom of the page write down your word that surmises your book. It can be anything: war, peace, love, frogs, anything. If you're typing your manuscript, open a new Word or Openoffice document and write your word at the end of the page.

Now set your timer for five minutes, go back to the top of the page and write to the last word.

If you do this, you will be writing a cracking ending any writer will be proud of.

Let me give you an example of what I mean. For those of you that have seen the movie Apocalypse Now, you'll know exactly what I mean, for those of you that haven't; you'll just have to take my word for it.

The last word at the end of the movie was horror. ***"The horror...the horror"***

The whole movie is about horror, the horrors of war, the horrors humans inflict on each other, how the soldiers deal with the horror. With the movie ending with the word horror, it ends very appropriate for the movie due to horror being the movie's topic.

So if you can end your book on word that summarises your topic, you're on to a winner.

The conclusion

This chapter is an extremely important part of your whole book writing experience, if you don't completely understand the techniques and strategies I've mentioned here go back and read the chapter again until it sinks in.

As soon as you've done the first few blueprint chapters, you'll find it much easier to do and you'll be able to do it on autopilot. Soon you'll be writing books faster than you ever thought possible.

In the next chapter I'm going to discuss the basics of writing a best seller, that's for both fiction and non-fiction. You'll discover how easy it is to write one and wonder why you haven't already. This is an exciting one, so please, keep reading.

Chapter 8

Writing your bestseller, whether it's fiction or non-fiction.

Now for those of you that want to go down the more traditional way of publishing, by getting an agent to represent you, here's a word of warning.

Unfortunately it happens, but a lot of agents reject manuscripts. I've had a few of students attending my workshops come to me and tell me their manuscripts keep on getting rejected by agents, and to be honest, I've been in the same boat. So I decided to do a little research for myself and asked a few agents why this was the case? Now this isn't because their writing is bad, in most cases it's incredibly good. Most of the agents that I had the opportunity to speak to say the reasons so many people writing fiction got rejected was, because the plot was, well, rubbish. In the case of non-fiction, it's because a lot of writers write about the same thing, but don't have something new to bring to the table. Look at it this way; a publisher has a book on weight-loss for new mums. They plough thousands into marketing and development, the last thing they need is another book about new mums losing weight that's exactly the same as the last one.

So for you to not get sent to the rejection pile, you need a best-selling plot for fiction and to come up with something new for non-fiction.

Let's start with fiction first.

Now perhaps you've had this great idea for a book swimming around in your noggin for some time now, you dream about it, and you may have spent years trying to develop it.

Good for you, but, I have to be brutally honest, if you don't stick to certain guidelines; it'll never end up on the bestsellers list.

One of the best pieces of advice I can give you is that if you feel you have a bestseller in your head; keep it for the third or fourth book. The sad fact is most first time writers, unless you're incredibly talented and lucky, won't produce a bestseller on their first try. The reasons for this are quite simple. Firstly, you are an unknown. Nobody knows who you are at the start, unless you're willing to fork out thousands to a publicist. Secondly, it's highly unlikely that the plot you are thinking about will amaze a traditional publisher. So for these reasons, I'd sit on the idea for a bit, at least until you have a few dedicated readers under your belt. However, we are living in modern times and the traditional publisher has most definitely taken a back seat to the more modern digital self-publishing. This is good news for you, because with a little savvy marketing, you could have a bestseller right of the bat, if you're lucky enough.

The best way however, to get a bestseller right out of the starting gate is quite simple. Go to the shop and buy yourself one. Now before you think I've gone off the rails, what I mean by that is go to your local used bookshop and buy a book that has already been a bestseller in the past. It stands to reason that if a book was a bestseller 8 years ago, it should still be a bestseller today, right?

Now I'm not saying you go out, buy a book that was a bestseller and copy it word for word. All I'm saying is you're going to get a book that you can borrow the idea from, and write a book of your own based on that idea.

Now before choosing your book, there are certain criteria that you need to follow.

Firstly, you need to make sure it's a fiction book you choose, it can be in any genre, pick a genre you'll be comfortable writing. Then it must be preferably between three and six years old. Three years so the plot is old enough to be out of memory and six so it's still relatively current.

Next, somewhere on the cover, it needs to say that it was either a national or international bestseller. Be careful not to choose a book that states: "By the bestselling author of..." The book you want to buy needs to be a national or international bestseller.

So what does that tell you? It tells you that firstly, the agent, editor or publisher thought it would be a bestseller and more importantly, when it hit the bookshops, it sold enough to become a bestseller.

Let me tell you a little something about publishers. They're a bit of a lazy bunch, if they could publish the same book that was a bestseller last year, with a different cover on, they'd do it. You know why? Because they know it'll be a bestseller again and they didn't have to work hard for the profits to come rolling in. Digital bookstores like Amazon and iBooks work on the very same principal.

The truth is the way they make money is by selling the same type of books year in, year out. So if you're holding in your hand a national or international bestseller, you're holding the key to your publishing success and the profits that come with it.

If you can't afford a new book, then take a look at Amazon.com. They have a variety of used books relatively cheap. Haven't got a computer? Go to the nearest car boot and pick yourself up one for a few pence. Alternatively, do it free, and go to your local library and pick one up.

So, in your hand is a bestseller, take it home and firstly read it from cover to cover. Once that's done all you need to do is, instead of writing a blueprint and then the book, reverse engineer it and write the blueprint from the bestselling book.

Once you have the blueprint of your book, simply start to write it using the techniques I've already shown you.

As I mentioned earlier, this doesn't mean you literary write the same book, use the blueprint to write your own book. Change the names, places or time. If it's an action, turn it into a thriller. If it's a crime drama, turn it into a horror. If it's a period drama, make it modern. If it's based in space, make it here on earth. If the lead role is a man, make it a woman. I'm sure you get my drift, just change as much as you possibly can, but keep the story and plot.

This happens nearly every day. Ever read a book and said to yourself, "this is the same as such and such." I bet you have.

For a perfect example I am going to use Roland Emmerich's Independence Day and H.G Wells' story War of the Worlds. Both had aliens in them that attacked earth, except in War of the Worlds they were called Martians. In both stories, the army uses tanks and bombs to try and kill them, but it doesn't work, except in Independence Day, they use more modern equipment and planes. Finally, in War of the Worlds they die because of bacteria. In Independence Day, it's because of a computer virus.

So, when thinking of a best-selling plot, you don't have to reinvent the wheel, just pick a plot that the public has already liked and brought.

Now on to Non-Fiction.

In most cases, the non-fiction book you want to write has already been written. So you need to create a book that's as good as any out there, but has new information that's presented in a way that excites the reader.

Here's what you do.

Grab yourself a few different books on the same topic that you want to write about, again, try between three and six years. If by chance there is a topic that you know hasn't been covered before, say "Looking after and caring for bright pink pygmy toads." Look for a similar book, for example, "Looking after and caring for amphibians". (Although, I wouldn't necessarily choose a topic that hasn't got a big following.)

Next, read through them and highlight the chapters that are relevant and necessary for your book. These would be the chapters that cover the same topic in all the books. You'll spot them as you go along.

So if your reading about a book on caring for amphibians, you'll get a chapter on feeding, one on breeding, one on supplements, one on habitat, etc, etc. Those are the exact same chapters you should have in your book. The simple reason for this is because your publisher and your reader will be expecting it in your book. You can certainly explain them in a different way, but the same chapters in the other books, need to be the ones you put in yours. This should give you a fair amount of the book already.

Always keep in mind though, when the reader buys your book, he's looking for a solution to a problem. Let's have a look at the amphibian problem. There could be number of reasons why the reader wants to learn about amphibians. He wants to keep frogs as pets, he wants a job at a zoo looking after amphibians, but doesn't know where to start. If you can present a solution to his problem, in a logical step-by-step manner, that he can follow easily, then you have a sellable book.

The next step is to create your own new and unique chapters. You want to bring something new to the table, possibly a new and unique twist to already used information.

For instance, if you're a breeder of poison arrow frogs and you have developed a new vivarium that emulates their environment better than anyone else out there, you need to add it to your book.

If you've had a new breakthrough in your field of expertise, this should be in your book. However, repackaging the same material in a different style could be just as effective.

Another way to create new or unique chapters is to simplify the complex. Are there ideas in the books you read filled with complicated jargon that you understand, but beginners may not? If you simplify the jargon and make it readable for anyone to understand and enjoy, then you create new chapters. So instead of a book called "Caring for Amphibians." You can have one called, "The beginners guide to caring for Amphibians."

If you simplify you book so anyone can read it, you have a different book from the rest of the pack.

Offering freebies to send them to your back end.

This is a favourite technique used by Internet Marketers that works really well.

At the end of your book you could have a free report that is worth, say £47, but costs nothing to produce. At the end of the free report you can offer them other services or another product, creating more profit for yourself. Or you could offer a free downloadable e-book that compliments the book you have written for their name and e-mail address. Once you have them on your list, you can set up an autoresponder and frequently send them other promotions and products for them to buy. Just make sure they can opt out of your e-mails to avoid being called a spammer. There are many ways you create different profit streams from your book, but that, I'm afraid, is for another book. Remember what we talked about in creating topics?

Get Testimonials.

You see them in almost every book, more often than not at the front. The more respected the source of the testimonial, the better.

Here's how to get them.

By now you should know who your target audience is. Think of between 10 to 30 names your readers "look up to". This can be a celebrity or someone who has already written a book about your topic.

Send them a cover letter and ONE chapter. If you send the entire book, you'll probably get a reply saying their schedule is full. Tell them that you value their input or comments and provide a separate piece of paper with a self-addressed envelope for them to put the comments on. If they give you a testimonial, that's great, but for the time being you just want their comments (basically, you want to see if they've read your work.)

After a week or so, send them another letter asking for a testimonial. Remind them of what your books about, what benefits it has for the reader and everything they need to give you a glowing testimonial. If you have testimonials from other people or celebrities, let them know who they are, as well as the celebrities you think are going to give you a testimonial. If you have a testimonial from a friend, make sure you tell the celebrity they are an expert in the topic of your book.

If you require a testimonial from me, just send me an e-mail to support@simplewritingstrategies.com with the headline can I have a testimonial please, with a brief synopsis of your book and I'll be happy to write you one.

If you want, make it easier for them and write your own testimonial you want for your book and tell them this is the kind of testimonial you want. It wouldn't surprise me if they just send it back signed. Make sure you have two copies, one for you and one for them.

In the next chapter I'm going to talk about research, how to drastically reduce you research time, how to interview the experts for research and much, much more.

Chapter 9

How to research your book in as little time as possible, giving you more time to concentrate on writing your book.

In this chapter you'll discover revolutionary techniques that will cut your research time to a bare minimum. You'll find out where and when to do your research, getting an answer to any question you may have in minutes and how to get the information no one else has that will make your book totally unique.

Now you could be an expert in your field, however, you don't know everything there is to know on your subject. There may be a few things that you need to research to make your book as accurate as possible. For the fiction writer, you may be writing a historical novel, well you'll need to do research to make your book as accurate as possible. Perhaps you are a crime writer, to make your book believable, you may need to research police tactics and strategies to make your book authentic and stand out from the rest of the crowd.

Whatever it is, this is what this chapter's dedicated to.

One of the biggest problems when it comes to your research.

I've found this time and time again. When people start researching, they find they research too much. They spend hours upon hours in the library or on the Internet, scrolling through pages and pages trying to get the right research, and they just can't seem to stop. As soon as they find one piece of information, they find another correlating piece of information and another, and another. They get tangled up in the fascination of it all and never get round to actually writing their book.

Don't get into that habit, and if you're already in the habit, stop it right now.

All you need to research is the answers to the questions you don't know about. It's as simple as that. As soon as you have the answer you need, move on to the next question.

Cutting the research process to a bare minimum.

So by now you already have the chapter blueprint in your book right? Now because you know exactly what's going to happen on every page in your book, you're most likely going to know what you need to research, what questions you need answers to.

So, say you need to do some research for chapter 3, question 10. (Remember the writing technique in the previous chapter?) Start your book answering your 15 questions of your blueprint for chapters 1 and 2. Answer all your questions in chapter 3 until you get to question 10, where you need to do the research.

By now you should have an idea on what needs to be researched. Write down a series of questions you need answering. Once you have the questions, you can go to your research source with the specific questions you need answering and find them without overdoing your research. Remember, you only want the answers to the specific questions you've raised.

For example, in your blueprint for chapter 3, question 10 is this: "What is the gestation period for a female green iguana?" The research you need to do in this instance is quite simple. All you need to know is how long a green iguana is pregnant for. So jot that on a piece of paper, go to your research source (a little on that later) find out the gestation period and make a note of it. Then, with the newly acquired information in the front of your mind, set your timer to five minutes and start writing. Do not think, and write the way you talk. Write as fast as you can. The faster you write, the better you write. Once the timer is finished stop, go to the next question.

This way, you only research when you need to and only what you need to.

The next bit of research you need might only be required when you get to chapter 12. If that's the case, continue to write your book until you get to chapter 12 and repeat the process.

Don't do all the research at once, research when you need it. If you do all the research at once, firstly you may find yourself falling into the trap of excessive researching and researching what you don't really need. And secondly, by the time you get round to actually implementing your research, you would've forgotten what you've researched and will have to spend valuable time reading up on it again.

You'll never ever see a chapter in a book called: Things I researched but didn't put in the book. You won't get credit for the research you've done but didn't use in your book.

The last thing you want to do is waste hours on end researching for something that you're just not going to use in your book. So please for your own sanity, just research the things that you're going to need in your book, and research it only when you need to, or when the book requires it.

But I want to write a historical drama. How can I write it without doing excessive research? The plain answer! If you don't have most of the detail rattling around in your head, don't write it.

It's true for certain types of book, to keep its authenticity; you need to do a lot of research, especially period dramas. You need to get the clothes right, the language and speech they use, all sorts of things. So unless you already know how they dressed and spoke like in the late 1800's, don't attempt to write it. At least wait until you have a couple of book under your belt, and you're a little better known and have the time to do the research. Also, always keep the readers needs in mind, if they read period dramas, then they will notice when the writer is bumbling through the book, the result will be you losing a valuable customer for your future books.

Using your own background to limit research.

When people ask me about what I think they're first book should be about, I always tell them to write a book based on their own experiences. If it is a non-fiction book, I always ask them what their profession and their passion are. If it's fiction, I ask them what their favourite genre is.

Writing from your own experiences usually cuts your research down to a bare minimum. You already have all the information stored in your brain, and you'll have some sort of idea on how you want to present the information.

All you have to do is firstly create a list of all the things you know about the topic. These are the things that you naturally know about and come to the forefront of your mind as you start to list them. Next start listing the things that you probably know, but aren't too sure about. As you start to list these, you start to realise there's actually more than you know. Lastly, list all the things you need to research, this should be a very small list.

Once this is done, look at your list as a whole and begin to formulate your chapter overviews by listing the 18 points you want in your chapters, crossing off the information on your lists as you go along. Once all this is done, start on your chapter blueprint.

If you don't know what I'm talking about here, I suggest you go back to chapter 7 and re-read it until you fully understand the concept.

The various research sources.

When you think of the modern ways you can research, the Internet immediately springs to mind. Yes, the Internet is a powerful way in which you can do your research, but the Internet is such a vast source of knowledge, you can end up spending hours looking for exactly what you want. There are a few alternative ways to get the exact research you are looking for without spending hours in front of the computer. I hope you decide to take notes, because this could be the difference in spending months writing your book, and weeks.

The Library.

So you pretty much know almost everything that needs to go in your book, but there will be a few things that you need to either clarify or research.

The library is one of the best places to do your research. However, as you walk in to your local library, instead of walking straight over to the adults' section to find what you are looking for, go to the children's section.

This particular type of research works extremely well for non-fiction. In the children's section you will find a plethora of books written on every subject imaginable. One of the best reasons why you should look at children's non-fiction books is because experts in their field have written them. How come? Because only an expert can write a book on a complex subject like Einstein's Theory of Relativity, and writes it so a six year old can understand. And if a six year old can understand it, then you certainly can. What's even better is they're extremely easy to digest, as they're only between 20 and 50 pages long. What you have in your hands will be a compact book with the essential information that can be easily read and understood by anyone. Remember what I said about writing as you speak? You can easily grab 20 or so books on your chosen subject and fly through them in under an hour, compared to the hours you can find yourself looking though the massive volumes of the adults section. In fact I urge you to completely forget about the adults section, this will only lead to excessive researching that you definitely don't want.

This strategy has helped me on numerous occasions and you'll be totally blown away at how effective this really is.

Remember though, you need to have your specific questions at hand so you know exactly what you're looking for.

Find an expert to tell you what you need.

One of the best ways of researching is finding and expert who has been there, done that and brought the t-shirt.

Firstly you need to find the expert. You can do this by searching your topic online. Go to **Amazon.com** and find books within your field, once you have someone in mind, see if you can find their contact details or contact them via the publisher. Then there are the children's books I mentioned above. Find the expert and, again, contact them via the publisher.

Explain that you are writing a book in the author's field of expertise and you would like to ask them a few questions on the subject. As soon as they say yes, which they invariably will, explain that you're **not** an expert – even if you are, and would love to pick their brain. The reason you say you're not an expert but are interested in the subject is because they immediately want to tell you everything there is to know on the subject.

The reason they normally say yes is because they love talking about the thing they are passionate about. Unfortunately their friends and family members are sick and tired of hearing what they have to say, so a fresh pair of ears to them is just what the doctor ordered.

Next, ask them what time would be best for them, tell them it shouldn't take more than 10 minutes of their time, even if it might take longer, you don't want to scare them off.

Remember – always have your questions at hand before the call. The last thing you want is them waffling on about things you don't really need. If you have the questions at hand and ask them directly, it cuts out the waffling process. If you find they do waffle on a bit, politely interrupt with another question you need answering. Soon you'll have all the questions you asked answered in record time, cutting the research process down to a minimum.

Record your interview with them. The best way to do this is if you use Skype. There's a piece of software called Pamela for Skype. You can download a free version that allows you to record up to 10 minutes of a chat. By recording the interview, you can always go back and listen to what was said and you don't have to frantically write everything down.

The Power of the World Wide Web.

With technological advances exploding since the early nineties, it's not surprising to know that the Internet is one of the best places to go to do research. But, it is vast and you can easily be sucked into doing more research than is actually needed.

That is why I always recommend you research only when you need to and have the questions to the specific problems you need resolved.

The first thing to do is go to good old Google, the largest Internet search engine, and type in the question as you have written it down. Now comes the hard part, sifting through the volumes of pages to get the answer you want. Firstly, always try sites like Wikipedia or Yahoo answers. If these fail to turn up any relative answers, just scan through the pages reading the information Google provides on the front page. Find the site that will most likely give you the answer you are looking for and open the page. If you've already written the questions down, you'll easily be able to find what you're looking for without much searching.

Another way to find what you're looking for on the Internet is by logging onto forums in your particular field and asking the question directly to the members. The only problem with this is, it can take a few days to respond, but you should get the answer you require. Simply explain that you're writing a book on the subject and you need a little help. You'll be surprised at the number of people willing to put their two cents worth in. I would only use this type of research as a last resort, as you can get far too many responses, all different.

Then there is Facebook. Facebook has grown astronomically over the last few years. Everyone who is anyone is on Facebook nowadays. To find the answers you need, go to search for groups within your chosen field or topic. No doubt you'll be able to find at least one group or fanpage. Once you have found the group join it and send a message to the wall, saying you are writing a book on that topic and you would like to interview an expert in the field. When you start to get responses, and you will, check out their profiles. If you think they have what you need, write the individual a note, just like the one you did when finding an expert. Try and set up a Skype meeting, get your questions in order and remember to record the interview.

The one question you need to ask to get the best answers possible.

Whether it is interviewing experts, reading books, developing your own strategies or verifying the information, you always need to ask yourself this question.

How will this affect my reader? That's the whole point of writing your book.

You have to tell your reader why the information is important to them. Why it will lose them weight, why it will make them more money, why it would save them on electricity bills. It's not always easy to ask yourself that constantly while doing research, but if you do, you'll be tapping in to the heart of your reader's motivation for buying your book and opens them to the idea of buying more of your books or services.

Now that you have learnt all there is to teach you about research, in the next chapter, we'll be talking about how to perfect what you have written, making it the best it possibly can be, through clever editing. Yes, you don't have to pay thousands of pounds or dollars to get your work professionally edited. You are perfectly capable of doing it yourself, find out how by turning the page.

Chapter 10

Now the book is complete, time to smooth it out with some savvy editing.

It's true that editing can make a good read, a great read. That's the intention you should always keep that at the back of your mind. You want the reader to hang off your every word. Editing doesn't have to be difficult at all and I'll show you some great strategies that I've learnt over the years that'll improve your writing.

Why you need editing.

When you sit down to write, you always want to convey excitement and reading ease. Those are the key aspects of editing and what editing is all about. Whenever someone asks me what editing is, I reply by saying that editing, in its essence, is the elimination of unnecessary words. Ask any editor what are the fundamentals of editing and they'll tell you the exact same thing, the elimination of unnecessary words. The excitement quickly fades when there are too many unnecessary words. When you cut out the unnecessary words you'll find your writing becomes much tighter and precise. Every writer must try to get the message across to the reader with precision. If you find that hard to do, then you've failed.

Now I know what you're thinking. "I've written the book, why should I edit it? Surely that's down to the agent or editor?" Well, I've got news for you, agents don't edit. If they have time, which is very rare, they might make a few suggestions, but that's it. All they have been tasked to do is sell your manuscript to the publishers. And if they don't approve your work, it won't get to the publishers editor. Even if you decide to self publish, the printing house has the right to refuse to print shoddy work. So it's in your best interest to get it polished up before submitting it to agents or publishers. Besides, you don't want to lose readers due to a poorly edited book, do you?

Hopefully, if you've listened and taken my strategies to heart, you may not need to do a lot of editing. Yes, I'm going to say those words again and they will probably be the last words I speak on my deathbed. The faster you write the better you write. And if you write fast, you'll write the way you speak, which means you'll be speaking directly to the reader. Also you won't have time to write long convoluted sentences and big words your readers won't understand. So it stands to reason that the quicker you write, the less editing you will need.

When you edit, you must always have the reader in mind. Ask yourself this question as you go along. **Is the message I'm trying to get across to the reader clear? Can it be made any clearer so it's easier to understand?**

If we think about fiction, you better make the story captivating, keeping the interest of the reader on every page. As you go though the editing process, always wonder if the story is entertaining enough for the reader. This thought should be constantly on your mind.

For non-fiction, make sure you give the reader all the information you said you would give them, never leave anything out and make sure the information delivers when the reader implements it for themselves.

Forget about Perfection.

No matter how much you edit, you will never get it perfect. Those who strive for perfection, never get their book published. You can certainly make it better, but never perfect.

So if you are a perfectionist, like I've said before, you better get over it. The sooner you realise that, the better.

There'll always be ways to change and alter your writing. I often find that when I return to one of my books, I can always make a few amendments here and there. But would it have been for the better? Maybe – maybe not.

Everyone wants their work to be as good as it possibly can be, but there comes a time when you have to stop, or you'll be changing things just for the sake of it.

There's a time in every book writers process where you'll say to yourself, "this is good enough." It may not be your best writing, but it's certainly not your worst.

So although there is a need for editing your book, you need to know when enough is enough.

Only edit after you've written your book.

I say this with the greatest of conviction, write you book first, and then begin to edit. Don't fall into the trap of editing after every paragraph or chapter. Your main objective is to get the words onto paper, write the entire book. The editing process should just be an afterthought. Write the book first, and then make it better.

When I first started in my writing career, I was obsessed with editing after every chapter. Guess what happened? It took me days to edit to get it perfect, yet it wasn't and was never going to be, and secondly I soon lost interest in the writing process and gave up for a whole year. Don't let that happen to you. In the beginning focus solely on your writing, keep the enthusiasm going and keep sight of the finish line. When it's all done, stick it in a drawer or put it in a folder on your computer and leave it for a few days. Then go back and start the editing process.

How long should it take to edit?

How long is a piece of string? There's no definitive answer to that question, however, going on my own personal experiences, I would recommend spending between 15 and 30 minutes on a chapter. It should take you an afternoon for a non-fiction book and just over a day for a large fiction book.

Try to restrict yourself to these time limits. The purpose of editing is to clean up your work and make it tighter, not to fully re-write your work.

You may feel that you want to give your work to a professional editor to edit it for you. If you want to, by all means do so. However, a word of warning, professional editors aren't cheap. Make sure you do your research on them before you hand over your heard earned cash. Personally, I feel you've already written your book, in my eyes, that makes you more than qualified to edit your own work. You're more than capable of doing it yourself.

However, in saying that I have specifically struck a deal with my sister company **frompen2print.com** to give you a great deal on editing if you feel you cannot do it yourself.

Just pop me a support e-mail with the heading "Help with my editing" to get a 30% discounted the off the website price.

Getting your computer to do all the hard work for you

For those of you that have written your book shorthand, firstly congratulations on completing such a mammoth task, your hand must be aching by now. Secondly, you've made editing a lot harder for yourself I'm afraid.

You'll find that most of your editing can be done with a few keystrokes on the computer. Here are a few ideas on how to make your writing tighter and read better.

Most computers have the find and replace tab. To bring it up, just hold down the Control button "Ctrl" and the F at the same time. Found it? Great!

Now see if you can replace every "the" with "your". If the sentence makes sense, change it.

Replace "have to" with "must."

Find every "that" and see if it can be removed.

Nearly every sentence containing "is," "are" or "am," can be easily re-written to remove these versions of "to be."

If a word ends in "ly" it's virtually always an adverb. Try to remove it and replace it with a stronger verb.

Try to get rid of adjectives and make your nouns more accurate or stronger.

Search for weak words like "almost, nearly, about, etc," and try to get rid of them to be more accurate.

Find phrases like "I am" and shorten it to I'm. "Have not," can be shortened to haven't, etc.

If you follow these simple computer edits, you may find this is all you need to do to tighten your work to an acceptable level. So take it seriously, because it's important.

Now it's time to kick your editing up a gear. The techniques I'm going to show you now will tell you whether or not your work requires any further editing. This starts immediately after all of your computer editing is done.

(F)irst numbering your paragraphs

This is going to seem strange but there is a valid reason why I want you to do this. Firstly, go to the back of your book and at the side of your last paragraph, put the number 1 next to it. On the penultimate paragraph enter the number 2 alongside it. Now working from back to front, number all your paragraphs through the entire book. You're very first paragraph should be the largest number. As you may have guessed, you're going to edit it backwards. The reason for this is I want you to evaluate all your paragraphs individually.

I find it easier to edit if I do it this way. Otherwise, if you edit each paragraph in order, you tend to look at the manuscript overall and get stuck in trying to perfect your work. Once you have finished numbering all the paragraphs, it's on to...

(A)dding up the numbers

Now I want you to read the first (last) paragraph and give it a score out of 10. Number 1 being the worst piece of drivel you've ever had the chance to read and Number 10 being Pulitzer Prize material. Don't be too hard on yourself, just be honest. The best way to do it is if you compare it to other work you've read in the same genre.

After you've scored all the paragraphs, add them all up and divide it by the number of your first paragraph (you're highest number.) You should now have a score out of 10. If it's any higher, you've done it wrong and you'll have to do it again. It's important, so take your time.

Once you have your score, if it's over 7, then my friend, you're manuscript is fine as it is. Can it be better? Most probably, but if it's over 7, then it will be ready for the agent or publisher as is, so there is no need to make it any better.

If you're book is lower than 7, then you have a bit of work to do. This leads me onto...

(S)tarting the actual editing process

So your manuscript has scored lower than 7 overall, don't despair, yes you have a bit of work to do, but it's not the end of the world.

Go back to each paragraph. If it scored higher than a 7, leave it alone. Again, can it be improved? Most probably yes. Is it worth the effort? No, not really, they're fine. Just leave them as they are. Remember, you want to try and make the editing process as quick as possible, so don't try to fix something that isn't broken.

Every paragraph that you scored a 3 or less, just get rid of, they're weak and will bring the writing down. Can they be fixed? Yes, most certainly. Is it worth the time and effort? Not really, do yourself a favour and get rid of them.

(T)ighten your work

The ones that are between 4 and 6 are the ones you'll be focusing on. All you need to do with these is tighten them so they get an 8 or 9.

Okay, the best way to show you how to do this is by giving you an example.

The Amazon River runs through the country of Brazil. It is home to many exotic creatures, including the infamous Piranha. It spans over 6200 kilometres. Along its banks live various tribes that depend on its water to survive. The Amazon Rainforest and its multitude of strange and bizarre residents also rely on the river to survive.

Okay, it's not the best paragraph in the world, but it's not the worst either. It needs to be improved. It currently consists of 56 words. All of them aren't essential.

The first part of the process is to pick out the essential words, like this:

Amazon River country Brazil home exotic creatures Piranha 6200 kilometres banks live tribes depend water survive Amazon Rainforest strange bizarre residents rely river survive.

Now the next step is to get rid of any redundancies. We know Brazil is a country, so we can get rid of the word country. We have already established that we're talking about the Amazon, so you can get rid of the word Amazon before Rainforest. Kilometres can be changed to km without losing its meaning. We can lose the word strange because strange and bizarre have the same meaning in this context.

Amazon River Brazil home exotic creatures Piranha 6200 km banks live tribes depend water survive Rainforest bizarre residents rely river survive.

Wow, we have just knocked it down from 56 words to 21. Now all we need to do is re-write the paragraph so it's a lot tighter.

The Amazon River in Brazil spans over 6200 km. Home to exotic creatures like the Piranha, its residents rely on it for survival.

Just 23 words, that's less than half of what we originally started with. It's now tighter and better written. You can see now why the basic robotic editing is so important.

After you've finished the four step process, you may find that the work doesn't flow as it should after you've edited it. This is where you use transitions (mentioned in chapter 7). All you need to do to bring your reader along is use the transition between the paragraphs and you're done.

A final word about writing, and editing with a partner.

A few years back, a very good friend of mine and I decided to write a screenplay together. At first we started to write it together, I was the better typist, so it was up to me to do all the typing. It started off okay, but soon we had conflicting opinions on what we wanted to happen. So, we decided to do a scene each. What a mistake. Within a week, he had finished his scene and gave it to me to edit and comment. I did the same. When we met again to see how it went, he totally butchered my scene, and guess what? I did exactly the same. This continued through the whole screenplay. Needless to say, it's sitting on my hard-drive doing nothing. Another fallout from the experiment is we aren't on speaking terms anymore, which is a shame, because if I knew what I know now, we would've made a really good team.

So how do you stop this happening to you?

Well, both of you can bounce ideas off each other and complete the blueprint. This doesn't actually require any writing. When it comes to the actual writing, each picks the chapters you feel comfortable writing. Since you've done the blueprint together, both of you know exactly what's going to happen in the book, but each of you are writing your favourite chapters. It's fine if your partner wants to read what you've written and vice versa, but for the love of your friendship, don't criticise or comment on each other's work. Edit your own chapters.

To make sure the book flows like is was one person wrote it, I suggest you hire an editor, or get another third person to edit your work.

Again you can get a discounted rate from **frompen2print.com** simply by sending me a support e-mail.

In the next chapter, I'm going to switch from talking mainly about non-fiction and focus on creating a mood with the power of suggestion. Now we're getting deep...

Chapter 11

Creating a mood with the Power of Suggestion and Colour.

Think of how you feel when you're writing or editing a certain chapter, how do you feel? Is it scared, sad, happy, or excited? You want your reader to feel that exact same feeling as you are, as they read your book. You'll want to strive to make the reader feel a particular way, whether it's disgust, anger, sadness, or happiness when reading your book.

Some writers spend hours writing, trying to get the perfect mood. Sometimes they never quite achieve it. So it's surprising to them to find out how you can create the perfect mood by describing human emotion and feelings.

Using the power of suggestion in 10 easy steps.

The subconscious mind is a very powerful thing. For years savvy advertisers and marketers have studied the human mind to manipulate the subconscious into buying their products. Back in the sixties the US government spent millions on developing subliminal messaging. Coca Cola also jumped on the bandwagon, getting people to buy coke by inserting flashes people drinking coke during film screenings. All of this is what's called "the power of suggestion".

Over the next few paragraphs, I'm going to show you a formula of describing and instilling feelings using the power of suggestion. The reader will begin to actually feel their heart racing or get a tingling down their spine. And no, it's nothing to do with mind control or subliminal messaging, if that's what you were thinking.

Any time an emotion is felt, whether good or bad, you can guarantee that emotion produces a physical symptom that is registered by a part of the human anatomy. Some emotions are internal, affecting the organs, while others are external.

For example: Anxiety can cause the stomach to tighten, causing physical discomfort, while exhilaration can cause your heart to pump faster, and the hairs on your body to stand on end.

The 10-step process I'm about to show you will help you to appeal to any human emotion, so you not only mentally stimulate your reader, but physically stimulate them as well.

Step 1

To inject a real feeling into your story, whether its fiction or non-fiction, you need to first identify the emotion you want your readers to feel. As soon as you know, describe it in a single word. Let's say you're trying to convey what a character felt. Ask yourself, "What single word captures what my character is feeling?
Once you have the word, write it on a scrap of paper.

Step 2

Okay, so now you have your word in front of you. Let's say for arguments sake, the word is "Cheerful." Below the word, write another 3 words to describe that feeling. I'm going to go with...

1.) Happy
2.) Smiling
3.) Uplifting

The reason behind choosing the three words is to become more familiar with that emotion. The more familiar you are with it, the better you'll write about it.

Step 3

Once you've written them down, choose the best one out of the three that you feel best describes that emotion. Can you see where this is going?

Step 4

Now I shouldn't need to tell you what to do next, but to make sure it sinks in here goes. Get a countdown timer and add 5 minutes. Starting with your chosen power word, attempt to describe the emotion you want to portray, make sure the remaining power words that you chose are in the first paragraph. Write as fast as you can for the 5 minutes. When the timer ends, stop writing. The faster you write the better you write. (I bet you're sick of hearing that?) If you are, good, it's sunk in. Don't try and make it too complicated, there's time to spice it up in a bit in the next few steps.

Step 5

Okay so now you have written your basic "feeling" paragraph. You've sort of created a basis on what you want your reader to feel. In this step and the next two, you're now going to add to basic feeling by adding three internal symptoms. Starting at the top of the body and working your way down.

Let's start with the mouth, throat, tongue, or ears.

The idea is to describe the sensations your character is feeling in their mouth, throat, tongue, or ears during the emotion you've already described. You don't need to use all the parts of the body, just pick the ones that best suit the situation.

So going on the cheerful emotion used above, you would perhaps say their mouth watered, throat tightened or their ears tingled or whatever?

Now take those feelings and write them just below the basic feeling paragraph and draw an arrow up to where you want to add them into the passage.

Give yourself around 3 minutes to figure out where you want them to go.

Step 6

Now it's time to move a little lower down to the cardio-pulmonary system, in other words the heart, lungs, and circulatory system.

So we know our character is cheerful because his eyes watered and his ears tingled. But what about his heart, did it skip a beat, did the blood rush through his veins, did his lungs want to burst through his chest?

Now do the same as you did above, write down the various cardio-pulmonary feelings and draw arrows up to where you want to insert them into the basic feelings passage. Again, give yourself three minutes.

Step 7

Moving even lower, we get to the gastrointestinal tract, the stomach and intestines. As you know, the stomach is one of the most sensitive parts of the body when it comes to feeling emotions. So it's always wise to use the stomach when describing emotions.

In my case, I think it would be safe to say that there were butterflies swimming around. In your case it might be different, maybe it's churning, maybe it's tied in a knot, whatever the case, give yourself 3 minutes and draw an arrow to where you want to insert it into the basic paragraphs.

Step 8

Right, now we're cooking on gas. You've got your 5-minute basic feeling paragraph, and then we went internally to describe what our character was feeling, starting with the head, moving down to the cardio-pulmonary system and ending up in the gastrointestinal tract. You've pointed out where you want the feeling to go in the basic feeling paragraphs.

Now it's time to go external, starting with the windows of the soul. I'm going to make my character wide-eyed with wonder. You can make them wide-eyed with fear, narrow angry slits, closed tight with fear, whatever your heart desires. Just make it relevant to the overall emotion your character is feeling.

As usual, give yourself 3 minutes.

Step 9

Moving swiftly along, along with the eyes, the other dead giveaway to what people are feeling are facial expressions, tone of voice and skin colour. Again, you don't have to choose all 3, just the ones that describe what your characters feeling.

I could say that my characters skin was glowing, or they had a smile as wide as a Cheshire cat or they're voice was shrill with excitement. Perhaps your characters nostrils flared, voice boomed, they were nervously biting their lower lip or their lips were pursed in a thin line.

Give yourself another 3 minutes to describe one or more of these external feelings.

Step 10

We can read a lot about a person just by reading their body language. I know exactly when my wife is fuming at me because she always turns her body away from me and folds her arms tightly, and of course, she refuses to speak to me. By describing your characters stance and body language, you can tell your reader quite clearly how they feel without them uttering a word.

My characters arms would probably be flailing excitedly and their legs twitching.

Your character could be clenching and unclenching their fists, or perhaps shifting uncomfortably in a chair, maybe they were shaking uncontrollably? Whatever your characters body language portrays, give yourself 3 minutes to describe it.

Bringing it all together.

Let's just quickly recap what you've done. You've written the basic 5-minute passage. Below it you've described 3 internal symptoms and 3 external symptoms, all with arrows pointing to where you want them to go in your basic feeling paragraph. This should've taken you around 20 or so minutes to complete. Now all you need to do is place the additions you've made in the appropriate place of your basic paragraphs.

The result being a "living, breathing" description of what your character is feeling. These feelings are then inextricably fed across to your reader through the power of suggestion, so they begin to feel what your character feels.

Have you ever gone to bed reading a really scary book? You get so engrossed that you are on edge. You start to hear things that aren't really there and get spooked when the telephone rings. That's more than likely because the writer has described the internal and external feelings of the victim cleverly.

If you can master the portrayal of feelings and emotions of your characters and project those same feelings onto your reader, you'll be on to a winner.

If you follow the 10 steps as laid above, you'll not go wrong.

How often should you do this throughout your story?

Normally after discussing the 10 steps to my writing workshops, I invariably get asked the question, ***"When and how often should I use a description of feeling during the story?"***

I normally put them in the story when my character is experiencing a really strong positive or negative emotion and you want your reader to experience it too. Whether they have just found the love or their life, or they are getting chased through darkened streets on a moonlit night. Whenever there is a full throttle ride of emotions that makes your reader feel happy, then angry, then disappointed, then exhilarated.

The best part is as you write it and read it back to yourself. You'll feel those emotions too.

Using colour to create a mood.

Picture this. You are painting a room and you have two shades of yellow in front of you. Puke yellow and sunshine yellow. Which yellow would you choose? I bet it's the latter. Yet when you think about it, yellow is yellow, but the connotations are very different. You wouldn't want to splatter your walls with puke yellow, yet sunshine yellow would positively light up a room. By adding different noun adjectives in front of the word yellow, you feel differently toward the colour. That's the essence of creating a mood.

In ancient Egypt, metaphysical practitioners used colours to affect their patient's moods. By simply projecting a certain colour onto a person's body, made them feel a certain way. There is no better way change a reader's mood, than with colour, or at least, particular types of colour. Let me give you an example:

"As Samuel passed the house, he looked up. In the top window was a figure looking out at him. The house had been empty for years now, but there, the figure was again. He glanced at the floor, and then, back at the window. The figure was gone."

Not much mood there, is there? In fact it's pretty bland. Let's have another look at the paragraph when I add a bit of colour.

"As Samuel passed the jet black house, he looked up. In the top deep black window was a figure looking out at him. The house had been empty for years now, but there, the black figure was again. He glanced at the ash black floor, and then, back at the dark black window. The figure was gone."

Spooky – right? Now let's change the mood again.

"As Samuel passed the rose pink house, he looked up. In the top sky blue window was a figure looking out at him. The house had been empty for years now, but there, the bright white figure was again. He glanced at the shiny black floor, and then, back at the window. The figure was gone."

It doesn't read as spooky anymore. In fact the bottom paragraph gives me a warm feeling while the top paragraph puts me a little on edge. Different colours and textures equal different moods.

Using different shades of colour can be the fastest way to change a mood in a story. And the best way to do this is subtly weave the different shades into a descriptive passage that evoke the desired feeling in a reader.

For instance, if you want your reader to feel nauseous, you would use the following descriptions for colour. Puke yellow, snot green, boil black, bile brown, etc.

If you wanted to create a dark mood for your book, you'll use colours like crimson red, jet black, ghastly green, midnight blue, etc.

Happy mood could be portrayed with descriptions like, sunshine yellow, beach ball blue, cherry berry red, bright white, etc.

To take your reader through a whole host of emotions you need to master the art of describing subtle shades of colour.

Some shades are perceived as happy, some angry, some sad, and some bad.

All you need to do is look the two examples above to know what I mean.

In order to get the desired effect you want your reader to feel, you must first understand that colour can affect a person's mood. Secondly, you need to know which colour provokes what type of mood or emotion. Third, you need to paint the scene with varying shades of that colour.

Below, I've accumulated the powers of different colours that affect certain emotions. This is very powerful stuff, so use wisely. **"With Great Power Comes Great Responsibility."**

BLACK

Black is a leading colour, it allows us to take control of any situation. It helps you face the fear of the unknown and boosts confidence. It strengthens your convictions and promotes self-control.

BROWN

Brown promotes stability and is useful in helping you make difficult decisions. It decreases mental activity, which when used properly, can bring your reader down from a heightened emotional state.

PURPLE

Purple has always been linked to spiritual awakening and inspires us to look to the heavens for guidance. It inspires creativity, strengthening the brain without exciting it. It's a very intuitive colour giving you a deeper insight. Purple makes you psychically sensitive.

ROYAL BLUE

Royal Blue has a tranquilising effect on the body while at the same time stimulates the mind. It's the colour of wisdom, contemplation and discernment. It creates a desire to know oneself, which can lead to great internal discoveries. It also has the ability to help a person appreciate the arts and finer things in life.

SKY BLUE

Sky Blue is the colour of intellectuals. This lighter shade of blue promotes a sea of tranquility. It inspires a feeling of trust, which enables the reader to listen better to the author. It's the colour of creativity, inspiring the creative spirit and increases perception. It enhances logic and analytical ability.

GREEN

Green has a nice calming effect. It calms the nerves and balances your feelings. It gives you clearer insight and gives you a feeling of tranquility. It also puts you in a practical state of mind and reduces eyestrain.

JADE

The deeper shades of green have a stronger calming effect and are excellent for calming nerves as well as leaving you with a carefree attitude. It promotes self-awareness and helps reader make internal discoveries about themselves. The muskier colours of green stimulate romance and idealism and are healing colours.

RED

Red is the most energising colour of them all. It's the colour you need when you're flagging and in need of an energy boost. It raises the blood pressure, gets the heart racing and makes you breathe faster. It creates courage and heightens sensations like enthusiasm, excitement, anxiety and expectation.

MAROON

Maroon can create a positive feeling towards yourself. It fills you with confidence. It makes you want to treat yourself to something nice. It can give you a carefree feeling as well as stimulate feelings of fun and sensual desire.

MAUVE

Mauve is a very soothing colour that relieves stress caused by confusion and worry. It allows you access to your intuition, making it useful for readers who need to solve a mystery. It gives you insight to the inner working of things.

PINK

Pink is a very soothing colour. It instantly calms you down and is a very loving colour. It encourages you to take a step back and look at things from a different angle, making you listen to your heart. It's used to soothe mental tensions and has the ability to make you accept new ideas.

ORANGE

Orange is an inspirational colour full of warmth. It can create impatience and restlessness, which can be used for both positive and negative results.

Orange can be portrayed as a clarifying colour. It helps to digest, transform and understand new concepts and ideas. It can help in organising your thoughts when a lot of information is thrown at you and gives you the get up and go so you get things done.

It's also a colour that stimulates appetite. Orange also helps you overcome psychological limitations you may have placed on yourself.

PEACH

Peach is not so much an energy boosting but an energy storing colour. It's a hybrid of orange and yellow, which inspires people to do more for the world they live in.

It evokes feelings of concern and clarity and promotes patience. This is an ideal colour to use when describing menial or repetitive tedious tasks.

GOLD

Gold promotes material security and motivates to high ideals. It encourages a person to reach for higher goals. It increases the appetite for material things, which is a fantastic motivator for achievement.

YELLOW

Yellow is a cheerful colour and a great anti-depressant. It's the happiest of all colours. It's the colour of spring, new beginnings and autumn, the beginning of rejuvenation. It helps with communication by getting one's point across effectively. It stimulates a desire for knowledge, which is fantastic if you want your reader to continue reading your book, because it spurs them on to receive the knowledge they're desperately looking for. It inspires optimism, renewal, rebirth and wisdom. It's a great colour for new beginnings and encourages tolerance.

SILVER

Silver enhances self-esteem and self-worth. It can overcome self-pity and gain hope to carry on. It's an inspiring colour that promotes a sense of honour.

GRAY

Gray alleviates stress, promotes relaxation and put a person in a passive state of mind. It's ideal for changing the mood from anxiety to a feeling of calm.

WHITE

White is the colour of truth, it inspires us to search for the truth and be honest with others and ourselves. It brings round a feeling of independence and is a great muscle relaxer.

It's also the colour of purity, putting a person on a higher plane of spirituality.

It's excellent for fighting negative thoughts by promoting optimism.

Lastly, it promotes open-mindedness, which is great for exploring the more unusual topics.

Wow, it got pretty deep there for a moment, nevertheless, time to soldier on in your quest to create the greatest book ever written.

In the next chapter we're going to talk about one of my favourite parts of the whole process – character creation. I'll show you a few simple steps that will help you create the vilest villain and the most heroic hero.

Chapter 12

How to create vivid and colourful characters, with a few strokes of a keyboard.

This is by far the best part for me, I just love the whole process of character creation, just knowing that people will love to hate someone that was a figment of my imagination, but to them, is a real life, living breathing person with flesh and bone.

Every time I hear someone say, "That so and so is a real nasty piece of work," or "wow, that detective of yours is a real nut-buster," it makes me feel all warm and fuzzy all over. But before I continue and let you in on the secrets I use to create my characters, let me first tell you...

The reason behind character creation.

The main reason behind character creation is to help the writing process move faster. The more you know about the character, the easier it will be for you and your reader to know exactly how they would react in any situation.

Now for a story to really jump out of a page, the characters have to be real people, the reader must think of them as a human being, with human emotions. When the hero gets hurt, the reader must feel for that character. When a baddie gets away with murder, the reader must have a feeling of shock, disgust and dismay.

The characters actions must also be consistent with what they've already done in the story. Let's say for instance, the protagonist you have in the story is a law-abiding citizen. He's a pillar in the community and is loved by everyone for the kindness he brings to others. Halfway through the story, you can't have him killing and eating someone's brains, it just won't sit well with your audience. The characters have to be consistent with their actions.

In saying that, you could show early on in the book, that the upstanding pillar of the community has a different, darker side to him behind closed doors. However, you need to show this early on so that the character remains consistent with his actions.

So the only way you are going to know their actions for sure, is to get to know them as well as you possibly can.

Now you can show the readers a few surprise characteristics along the way, after all, they don't know the character as well as you do, but as it comes nearer to the end of the book, they should know exactly how that character would react in a certain situation.

The plot can twist and turn in about every direction possible, but the characters must remain creatures of habit.

Put it this way, if you were put in a certain situation, and I asked your partner how you would react to the situation, because they know you so well, they'd know exactly how you would react, as would you. That's how you have to create your characters. By the end of the book, the reader must know them well enough that they will be able to predict what they will do in a certain situation.

For you to enable yourself to do this, you need to know everything about the character you're about to create. Who their parents were, where they grew up, how many brother and sisters they have, where they went to school. Basically what made them the person they are today. This is called "creating a backgrounder" and it's essential for making your characters as real as possible. More on this a little later. Now you know the reason why it's important for character creation, why not step into my little "Frankenstein" laboratory as I show you…

The easiest way to create a character.

You've probably thought of this already as you were reading the above. Anyway, the best and fastest character creation process in the whole world is basing a character on you and your own personality. You know everything there is to know about you. You know your quirks, your reactions, your personality, even your deep dark secrets. You have your whole life history. You know your parents, grandparents, and siblings. You know how they moulded you into the individual you are today. You know exactly how to react in any given situation. So it stands to reason, the easiest way to create a character is create one in your own image.

Every author writes himself in a book, you show me an author who hasn't and I'll show you a liar! It may not be the main character. It may be a supporting role. It may even be certain quirks or traits in several characters, but the author is definitely in the book.

So if you find yourself looking at the blueprint, thinking I would make a good character, don't fight the feeling, embrace it and become that character, your writing will be much stronger for it.

Whenever my wife reads one of my books, she always knows exactly who my character is, firstly because she knows the way I act, and secondly, it always reads a little bit better than the rest.

Some more ingenious ways to create the ideal character.

Once you have your first character, yourself. Again don't deny yourself. Put you in your book, you'll see its great fun.

Anyway, you have your first character, the next best thing is to use someone close to you, either your partner of a best friend, and someone you've known for years. Just make sure you change the characters name for privacy reasons. You know their personality, you know how they would react in certain situations, you would know the stance they would use, the facial expressions, what they'll wear, what they'll say.

I often put friends and acquaintances in my books. When I was a kid there was this bully in my school, he made a great antagonist. Not only that, it gave me great pleasure seeing him suffer him my book. I'm sure by now you can see how easy it is to create your characters.

Now you have a few more characters in your book, but you need just a few more. The next step is to use someone famous, someone you know. It can be a movie star portraying a specific role, a character from another book you've read, any personality you're familiar with. The whole objective is to know your character inside and out in the least possible time.

Last but not least, are use characters that have already been used. Remember we spoke about taking a bestseller, and re-writing it. Well, in this instance, you'll have all the characters set out for you. Nothing is stopping you from transferring an American war hero's personality onto an African goat herder or the traits of a female astronaut to a male deep-sea diver. Just by changing the plot as much as possible guarantees the fastest way to write your book on the planet.

Moving on to Non-Fiction characters.

An easy way to get the message across to the reader is by introducing characters to help convey the message.

They normally come in the form of homilies or parables.

"Let me tell you the story of Leigh-Anne, who wanted so desperately to lose weight so she could find her ideal man. It's the story of how she found motivation to lose weight and the problems she faced along the way. You'll find out exactly what diet and exercise regime worked for her and you'll soon realise that Leigh-Anne, is just like you. So you better learn her lesson well if you want to have the same success as she did."

This type of character can work really well for non-fiction books and can be used to its full advantage if you're familiar with the character. Maybe it could be you. Maybe it could be a family member or a very cleverly disguised fictitious character

Creating your own original characters.

It's always great fun when getting to create your own unique character. However, people often get a bit flustered when I ask them to tell me about the character they want in their book. Sometimes they simply don't know where to start. To me it's logical to start from the beginning, where they were born, or where they went to school or even what their favourite past time is. You don't have to know absolutely everything there is to know about the character. You just need enough to know how they will react in a certain situation within the story.

So let's get the electricity cranking through the Frankenstein character creation laboratory! **Whoa ha ha ha!**

First get a pen and paper, or create a new document on the computer.

Think of where you want your character to come from and just jot down where they were born, where they grew up, and their parents and siblings names. This is just a basic beginning to your character. Remember, the more you know your character and how they'll react to certain situations, the easier it'll be to write.

Now once that is done, give them a nickname. This might just be between you and the character; maybe it might come out early on in the book or maybe it something that your character does during the story for him to get it.

A nickname can tell you more about a person and a lengthy biography. It can tell you about a person's past, their flaws, failures ambitions and successes.

A nickname can change how you perceive that character.

Let's give you an example. Most of us know about the infamous gangster Al Capone. You

may know him as "Scarface." This immediately puts a negative image in our minds. What if his nickname was "sweets" or "bunny?" It immediately changes our perception of the man.

So give your character a nickname, it can be anything you want it to be. Can't really think of one? Just add an "s" to the end of a noun or adjective or add "the" at the beginning. Here's a few of mine I've been labelled with over the years. Bookworm, Bones, Werty, Penguin & Swifty.

The secret to creating a living, breathing, walking, talking character.

If you want to bring your character to life, you need a minimum of 3 personality traits. If you put the right ones next to each other, you'll have a description so vivid. The reader will see it as a human being.

With 3 personality traits the reader will be able to envision what they look like, how they dress, and how they developed the traits in the first place.

Look at the 3 personality traits I've created below. See if you can picture the people in your mind.

1.) Kind, Quiet, unsocial
2.) Tempermental, loyal, dangerous.
3.) sly, manipulative, friendly.

I bet if you close your eyes you would be able to picture each character, whether it be a man or a woman.

The reason I say at least 3, is because if you use one trait, it normally creates a cartoon character. Take the 7 dwarves for instance. If you use two, you normally describe a stereotype.

3 personality traits bring a character to life.

Now the problem that a writer faces is picking the correct traits to create your character. Don't worry, all will be explained below, including the 5 personality categories that human beings exist in and how to expand on each personality.

The 5 personality categories.

Although humans have a wide range of personalities, they can all be boiled down to their 5 categories:

1.) Very Good
2.) Good
3.) Normal
4.) Bad
5.) Very bad.

You can create an infinite number of characters with these main personality headings. However, as you'll soon find out, only 3 of those headings make great characters readers love. They're the good, normal and bad personalities.

The very good and very bad characters just aren't interesting enough. A very good character that never steps out of line, obeys the rules and never does anything wrong is, let's face it, very boring and not interesting at all.

When it comes to the very bad character, someone who has been spawned from the depths of hell, very few people can relate to them. Hopefully you're not one of them.

Another reason why super evil people aren't interesting is because your reader doesn't care what happens to them. At the end when the baddie is caught or killed, the audience just won't care, and if they get away with it, it'll just leave your readers angry.

Getting the "Personality Formula" right.

When working out your characters personality traits, if you follow this simple formula, you will be able to create any one of these five types of characters in a matter of seconds:

1.) Very Good – Two positive and one neutral trait.
2.) Good – Two positive and one negative trait.

3.) Normal – One positive, one neutral and one negative trait.
4.) Bad- Two negative and one positive trait.
5.) Very Bad – Two negative and one neutral trait.

It's easy to pick a positive or a negative trait, but neutral traits are a different kettle of fish. Neutral traits are traits that some would argue are positive, while others would argue as negative. They are normally controversial in nature.

If a trait is neither good nor bad, but "just the way the person is," then it's a neutral trait.

Controlling, for instance is a neutral trait. People who don't like being told what to do would find that negative, however, an individual who just likes to "go with the flow" would class it as a good trait.

Why give a good character a bad trait and vice versa?

It's simple, each of us is flawed, and it's how nature intended us to be. In a good character it will be that flaw that will be the negative personality trait. This is the trait that makes them exciting and get into situations they wouldn't normally get in, and is normally the trait that the reader relates to the most. As for the bad person having a good trait? It makes the reader become emotionally attached to the character. Readers always want to see the good in everyone and hope that that teeny tiny bit of goodness will shine through and make the character see the error of his ways. Also in the bad character, a good personally trait is often seen as the bad characters weakness. Therefore it's also a flaw.

Surprisingly, it's the normal character that is the most interesting. The normal character has a good, bad and neutral personality trait, making them highly unpredictable. They are normally the person next door. What makes them so exciting is no one quite knows how they will react to a situation. Another good thing about normal characters is every reader in the world will be able to relate to at least one or their traits.

Creating your characters personality.
Below you'll find an extremely simple method for creating your characters personality.

Using the same piece of paper or document you started creating your characters background, follow the formula below:

First you need to decide which of the 3 personality types you want your character to fall under. Once you know, write it down.

Once you have the general personality, (good, normal or bad), you need to come up with the right personality traits. So if it's a good character, you'll need to come up with 2 positive traits and one negative trait. A bad character should have 2 negative traits and 1 positive trait and finally the normal character should have one of each and a neutral trait.

And that it, that's all you have to do to create a living breathing character.

Okay, let me give you an example. Joe Bloggs is the protagonist in the story. He's a detective that's loyal and trustworthy, but he has a violent temper. So his 3 personality traits are: Loyal, Trustworthy, Bad temper.

Now that you have you character, close your eyes and see if you can picture them.

Adding more meat to the bones.

Okay so now you have the basics of a character, he has three personality traits, now it's time to build on that character. Now there are 5 steps or ingredients you can add to beef up your character. I'd advise you to add one of these "ingredients" at a time. The first step is absolutely crucial and must be added, step 2 helps with the reader's imagination and helps them picture your character, so I'll add that too. Every other stage is merely ascetics but isn't necessary.

Step 1

The first step you've already done, and that is selecting the 3 personality traits.

Step 2

This is the step where you add his or her habits and pet phrases. So what sort of habits do they possess, do they pick their nose, bite their fingernails, always double check the door before leaving the house? Human beings a creatures of habit and highly predictable, in what they do and say. Does your character have a particular saying? If so jot it down. A pet phrase is something they say more than once and it makes the reader know the character deeper. For example, "Yabba dabba do," or "Go Ahead! Make my day."

Step 3

This is where the hands and eyes come in to play. Over the centuries fortune-tellers have been able to read a person's personality simply by touching their hands. The softness or roughness of a hand can tell a lot about the person. For instance, someone who has soft hands probably works in an office, while rough hands can tell you a person probably works in a factory with his hands. The condition of the fingernails is also a good indication of a person's personality. When you describe your characters hands, you're subconsciously telling the reader about their personality.

When you start to describe your characters eyes, don't do what nearly every writer does and describe the colour. The eyes are the windows to the soul, so describe what the narrator or other person sees when they look into the characters eyes. Do they see deep sorrow? Or a twinge of insanity?

Step 4

Now we get to the clothing. What is your character wearing? Is he sharply dressed or does he wear shabby clothes? You don't have to go over the top and describe every little piece of clothing, just mentioning the shoes they're wearing or jacket can tell the reader a lot about that character's personality.

Step 5

Most humans have the same physical characteristics as we all normally have two eyes, two ears, a nose, two arms and two legs. For step 5 don't describe the normal characteristics, go for the unusual physical characteristics. For instance, does he walk with a limp, or have a speech impediment? How about giving your character a deformed hand?

Look for the more unusual characteristics that make them a little different from the rest or the human beings.

By the time you have described your character using the steps above, you should've given the reader a clear picture in their mind of what your character looks like and an insight to their personality.

You have just created a life, isn't it exciting? I hope that when you get to this part of the process, you'll have just as much fun as I do when creating characters.

In the next chapter we're going to learn about the next stage in the writing process, getting your work into print. I'll be discussing the 4 routes you can take to get published, getting an agent to sell your work to the publisher, cutting out the middleman and going straight to the publisher, then there's my favourite becoming your own publisher, and finally another favourite of mine digital publishing.

Chapter 13

Getting it to Print, exploring the possibilities of getting it published.

Okay, so now you have spent the last month or so writing and editing your book. What now? Well the whole point of writing it in the first place was to sell it right? In this chapter I'm going to show you the three routes you can go down to get your work published. I personally prefer the self-publishing route for my own personal reasons, however, to remain unbiased, I'll talk about going down the traditional route also. So let's begin with the, now ever increasing unpopular, traditional publishing.

The Agent

If you decide to go down the traditional route of publishing and this is your first novel, it's wise to seek out an agent to promote it to the publishers for you. The reason is simple. They are the professionals in the industry. They work daily with the publishers so they've built up trust with the publisher. You'll have a greater degree of success if you decide to go with an agent, because the agent's word is worth their weight in gold.

If a publisher was faced with two books to publish on the same subject, one written far better than the other one, but the one of poorer quality was suggested by an agent, what book do you think the publishers would decide to publish? It'll be the one that was suggested by the agent. The reason is simple. On the one hand you have a would-be author. A book written by a nobody, the publishers don't know if the book will sell or not, and they're likely to take the chance either. The publisher on the other hand knows the agent. They've worked on many successful and profitable projects together. So it makes sense to go with the agent's recommendation.

The initial query

So what's the agent looking for? Well, basically you need to write a cover letter to the agent or Agent's Acquisition Letter and they need a synopsis, a basic overview of the whole story. If the book is written, then 3 sample chapters will need to be sent along too. The synopsis will show the agent the whole book has been at least thought through, if not written entirely, and the sample chapters will show the agent that you can actually write the book. Your main aim is to sell the book to the agent first, before they put their reputation on the line and sell it to the publisher.

However, keep in mind, it can take several months for the agent to respond to your letter. They are very busy creatures and see thousands of proposals every day. So you'll need the patience of a saint. Also, I would recommend sending to as many agents as you possibly can. The last thing you want is to wait 4 months, get rejected for some reason, and then send another query letter to the next agent only to wait another 4 months.

The cover or acquisition letter

At the end of this book, I've provided you with a sample Cover letter or Agent's acquisition letter, including a dissection on why it works. By all means use this as a template for your own, if you want to try and get an agent to represent your work.

The synopsis

For the synopsis, whether it is fiction or non-fiction, you're going to write a single paragraph that summarises each chapter in your book. After each paragraph, you'll want about 4 bullet points of what happens in the chapter. The reason you do this is because you want the agent to have a really clear idea what's happening in the story, or in non-fiction's case, what information you'll be providing the reader. However, you don't want to provide too much information that the editor can find fault with it. You want to give them just enough information to make a positive decision.

For example, let's use the story of Goldilocks and the three bears again.

Chapter 1

Goldilocks is a young mischievous girl that decided to take a walk in the forest. After a while she comes upon a house in the forest. She's lured by the sweet smell of porridge and peeks in the window to see if anyone is home. After seeing it empty she steps inside for further investigation.

- An air of trouble and the promise of free food.
- The surreal setting of the house in the woods and the trouble that lies ahead.
- The curiosity of the young girl will eventually land her in trouble.
- The role the bears will play.

All you need to do is copy this formula for the rest of the book and you'll have your synopsis.

Okay, I know that's not how the story really goes, but hey it's a story remember.

You need to make each chapter synopsis so exciting and dramatic that it forces the reader to carry on, wanting to know what happens next in the story.

The 3 sample chapters

Now at this stage, it isn't necessary to send the 3 sample chapters, however, what I will say is, every agent is different, some expect the sample chapters with the initial query, and others may not need it straight away. Before you send off your initial query to an agent, always read their submission guidelines thoroughly. If you don't, you may face the rejection pile before it's even looked at.

In my personal opinion, I would send them regardless. You've written the book already, so why not give them a taster of what it's all about.

Now you can send any three chapters, it doesn't have to be chapters 1, 2, and 3. It can be 1, 6, and 10 if you like. What I would say is send chapter 1 as one of them. This will be one of your best, as you want to grab your reader right from the start. The other two can be the ones you find has the best opportunity to snag an agent.

After the initial query letter

Sometimes an agent will be happy with your initial query and take you on as a client straight away. If that's the case, congratulations! Sometimes, however, they need a little more to be persuaded. This is where the formal proposal comes into play.

Below is an example of how it should be laid out.

The title page
Book proposal
(Title of your Book)
By (Your Name)
(Your Address)
(Your Telephone number)
(Your e-mail address)
(The proposed agent's name)
That's it for the title page.

Overview

This is about one or two pages telling your reader exactly what the story is about. Leave no stone unturned, the reader will need to know every twist and turn in the plot, right up until the ending. As for non-fiction it's all the information you provide the reader and how they will benefit. If you like, you can use your synopsis.

Format

This is where you tell the agent or editor how the book will be presented. Don't get into specifics, like type styles, kind of paper, binding preferences and that sort of stuff. All they require is the number of pages, number of chapters, word count, if you're using illustrations or photos, that kind of stuff.

Market

This is where you explain who's going to buy your book and why. For non-fiction writers that should be simple, as you wrote your book with a specific type of person in mind. As for fiction, think of the genre and whom it will appeal to.

Be as specific as possible, for instance, what kind f people are they? What are the demographics? Give the agent as many reasons why these people will be running to buy your book.

Promotion

What will you be doing to make the book a success? Tell the agent what your plans for promotion are. If you haven't thought of this yet or thought that the publisher will be doing all the promotion for you, think again. Remember, there's no such thing as a best-selling book. You only have best-selling authors.

For better chances of acceptance, you need to show the agent and the publisher that you're willing to get your hands dirty and get stuck in. Make it known that you'll be trying to get yourself on radio shows, doing book signings and appearing on the telly. Tell them you're prepared to spend your advance on hiring a professional PR company.

Competition

This is where you'll have to do a bit of homework and find out what competition is out there. Tell the agent what books your book will be competing with. Provide the names, publisher, and ISBN. Then tell them why all of those suck compared to yours and why yours is so much better than any others out there.

However, don't mention books over 10 years old, they're simply not your competition.

Authors Biography

This isn't your life story. You don't want to bore them to death. (I'm not saying that your life is boring, you just don't need it here.) You just need to explain why you're an authority on the subject you've written about. It can be anything that will boost your credibility or your appeal to media.

Sample Chapters

If you haven't sent them in the initial enquiry, then you can send them with the formal proposal. Remember, these can be any 3 chapters. The purpose of these is to prove that you can write well enough and to a publishable standard.

That's it, that's basically how you formulate your formal proposal for the agent to review.

The Traditional Publisher

Some of you may feel that you want to skip the middleman and go straight to the publisher, after all you've done all the hard work in creating the book, why share 10% for everything you make.

The process for contacting the publisher direct is exactly the same as if you were contacting an agent. You'll need to supply a cover letter, a synopsis, and 3 sample chapters.

Again be prepared to wait a long time for a response. So send to as many publishers as you can.

The Pros and Cons of Traditional Publishing

The definition of traditional publishing is when a Publishing House signs you to a contract, gives you an advance, takes your manuscript, edits it to publication standard and gets it onto the bookshelves of stores.

Below is a list of things to consider when going down this route.

Pros:

• Kudos and prestige when published with a famous house.
• Professional editing, printing and distribution – all free.
• Easily accepted in bookshops and other retailers.
• Some marketing costs covered and you may get offered a publicist.
• An advance may be given on future royalties.
• May be offered a multiple contract if your books sells well.

Cons:

- Extremely long lead times – so be prepared to wait.
- Lack of control over the process and final product.
- If your books don't sell, you lose your contract and the books get destroyed.
- You only have a maximum of 3 weeks to make sales before your books get pulled off the shelves.
- You may have to pay back the royalties if unsuccessful.
- You have to aggressively and constantly promote to make sure you get sales.
- You lose all the rights to the book, so if your books don't sell well, you can't publish them elsewhere.
- Royalties aren't very good – only 3 – 5%.

Vanity Publishing

This is the type of publishing I personally, would avoid like the plague, however, for the benefit of my loyal readers, yes you, I'll discuss it briefly here.

Now there's a lot of similarities between Vanity and Self or Print On Demand (POD) publishing and a lot of authors, when starting out, get confused between the two. However, as I'll explain below, there are differences.

The Pros and Cons of Vanity Publishing

Vanity Publishing can be described as this: A Vanity Press or Vanity Publisher is when a Publishing House publishes books at the authors' expense. Or compiles a collection of short stories and sells them back to the author.

Pros:

- Author retains the rights to the book.
- Author has 100% creative control – you have the book the way you want it.
- Author sets his own discount and loyalty rates.
- It's far quicker than traditional publishing.

•	You don't have to worry about ISBN numbers, as they provide you with one.
•	Great sales and marketing tool – far better than a brochure.

Cons:

•	You don't get the acclaim of being a "published author."
•	If you use a known one, it kills you as an "authority" on a certain subject or niche.
•	You take all the risk and pay them the privilege.
•	The ISBN belongs to the publisher.
•	Book wholesalers and retailers don't like vanity books.
•	You have to do all the editing, typesetting and cover yourself.
•	It's very hard to recoup the costs involved with Vanity Publishing.

Yes, there are a few advantages it has over Traditional publishers; however, the disadvantages far outweigh the advantages. Don't despair though, because now we are going to discuss my favourite type and publishing and for good reason.

Self-Publishing

Originally this was going to be a chapter on it's own, but it seems silly to write different chapters on the different types of publishing when I can wrap it all in one neat little bow. Right? Moving on…
There used to be a time when self-publishing was frowned upon. Times have changed. I know a variety or authors that started getting published traditionally, but have now gone down the self-publishing route, and vice-versa. Some very famous authors that have self-published are: Beatrix Potter, Virginia Woolf, John Grisham, T.S Elliot, Rudyard Kipling, and the list goes on, this is just the tip of the iceberg.

With the boom of online bookstores, it's far easier now to get a best seller via self-publishing than with traditional publishing. As with everything there are pros and cons to both, which is discussed below.

The Pros and Cons of Self-Publishing

Self-publishing, also known as POD (Print On Demand) Publishing is the publication of any book or other media by the author of the work, without the involvement of an established third-party publisher. It's also done at the expense of the publisher.

Pros:

•	The author keeps all the profits.
•	The author is entitled to 100% of the profits from foreign and film rights as well as other media, (eBooks).
•	The author has complete creative control.
•	It's far quicker than traditional publishing and you print only what you need, keeping the costs down.
•	You still get the acclaim of being a published author.
•	Distribution is easy through online booksellers like Amazon and Barnes and Nobel.
•	If a traditional publisher wants to buy the rights, you don't have a contract to buy out of.

Cons:

•	The author takes all the risk, but it can be minimised.
•	You will need to sort out an ISBN number, editing, typesetting, production, publication and distribution. You are your own publisher. Some companies offer this service as extra. (See below for explanation.)
•	Hard to turn a rough manuscript into a finished product. (I've got you covered on this one.)
•	Can be challenging to get books wholesalers and retailers on your side, but it is getting easier.
•	Finding a good and freelance book designer can be difficult.

• You could have a difficult time getting it into bookstores.

So as you can probably see, there is similarities with Vanity Publishing, however, the two main differences are firstly, when you publish with a Vanity Publisher you pay the publishing house to publish your book, whereas when you self publish, YOU are the publisher, you only pay for the books that get printed. Secondly with Vanity publishing you don't get the acclaim of being a published author, whereas with POD, you do.

Digital Publishing

Over the last six years or so there has been a massive uptrend in authors going online and getting published digitally. This is all due to the rise in sales of e-reader devices such as Amazon's Kindle, Apple's iPad and Barnes and Nobel's Nook.
The way we publish and read books is changing rapidly. Bookselling is now moving online and replacing the old traditional "brick and mortar" stores. Reading is rapidly moving to screens as eBooks and is replacing print books.

The Pros and Cons of Digital Publishing.

Digital publishing is when you publish a book solely online. You can publish in a variety of formats such as .aeh, .cbr, .epub, .mobi etc. It's absolutely free to publish in digital format, all you have to do is upload your file to the distributor and you're good to go.

Pros:

• Author sets the price and keeps all the profits
• Extremely easy to publish with major distributors, just upload a file and you're good to go.
• Global distribution. There is absolutely no constraints when it comes to publishing so you can publish to anywhere in the world.

- It's free to get published. By uploading your manuscript yourself, and no costs to physical publishing, it's free to get your book published.
- It's super quick. As soon as you upload your book, it could be ready to sell within hours.
- The author retains all the rights to the book.

Cons:

- The author takes all the risks.
- The author has to do all the editing, formatting, typesetting, publication and distribution. (although some distributors will do this for a fee.)
- You have to get your book designed yourself.
- You have to do all the marketing and promotion for the book.

So why Self-Publish your own work?

Well there's a plethora of reasons why you should, but for now I'm going to give you ten great reasons why you should be the publisher of your book.

Time – Traditional publishing far takes too long, usually around 18 months. With Self-Publishing you could have your book in your hands within a month.

You get your book the way you want it. You get total control of the whole project, from start to finish.

You keep 100% of the rights – You own the content.

You can get to test the market – Find out how well it will sell & how successful it will be. Start small and then scale up.

If you have a limited market or niche it may not interest a large publishing house.

Legacy – your book is an expression of yourself & a great legacy to leave behind.

You get global distribution. – Amazon.com, Barnes and Nobel, Nielsen books, not to mention your local bookstore.

Digital Availability – You have the choice to also publish them as e-books to sell online or on the Kindle and other e-readers.

Promotion – There's a variety of cheap and effective ways now made readily available to promote your book into the stratosphere.

Instant credibility – You are seen as an expert.

POD Services

Most self-publishers offer a wide variety of services so you'll need to pick the one that is right for you.

All of them should provide you with an ISBN number. Availability in online bookstores like Amazon and Barnes and Nobel, a choice of sizes, binding, type fonts etc and a free copy to make sure everything is to your approval. If they don't provide these basic needs, then find a publisher that does.

Again, I have struck up a deal with out sister company **frompen2print.com** to give you the best deal on the net.

However, just to show you I'm not biased, I've supplied some names and web-addresses of some other self-publishing companies in the final module.

Traditional Versus POD Publishing

Now here are a few things you might not know about publishing, consider this food for thought.

In 2011 a total of 288,355 books were traditionally published in the U.S compared to 764,448 self-published books. (Bowker.com). That's a massive 4:1 ratio.

Due to the digital age, it's harder to get Published Traditionally, hence the uptrend in previously Published Authors now going down the Self Publishing route.

It's far easier to go Digital via Self Publishing than Traditional Publishing. In fact, in most cases, Self Publishing houses offer an e-book service as standard. Some go one step further and offer your book as an App that can be downloaded from iTunes. Both are offered at frompen2print.com. Historically Traditional books received better marketing than POD (Print on Demand) books. However, it has now become far easier to promote POD books due to Social Networks like Facebook, Twitter and Pinterest.

In 2011, there were more Self Published Books sold on websites like Amazon, Barnes and Nobel and other online bookshops than Traditional Books.

You have a better chance of getting Published Traditionally on the back of your success as a profitable Self Publisher.

Finally, as mentioned above, Rudyard Kipling, Ernest Hemingway, Steven King & Mark Twain – these are just some of the big names who started off their careers in Self Publishing.

The Digital Publishing Era Has Well And Truly Begun.

There's a whole range of new publishing and distribution tools available today that now empower the author to become their own publisher. Now digital publication has allowed the author to go global with no constraints and finally, digital publishing is kind on the purse strings, in fact it costs absolutely nothing to publish your book digitally.

So it stands to reason that this should be, besides self-publishing in paper, your choice in publishing.

I have one word of advice when it comes to publishing digitally. Maximise your distribution.

When we think of digital publishing, most people think of Amazon Kindle, and there's good reason for that, as they have the lion's share of the US market in 2013 (around 60%. However, there's a plethora of other digital publishers out there, like Apple, Barnes and Nobel, Kobo, Sony, Flipkart and even Diesel. So when thinking about digital publishing, you want to publish on all distribution networks.

One way to do this is to use **smashwords.com** as your distributor. For a very small fee, they will distribute your book to all the digital publishers out there, except for Amazon.

The reason you want to do this is it takes a lot of hard work to publish you book to each distributor. Each distributor has there own formatting rules you have to abide by and keeping accurate records is a nightmare. Just remember, if you go down this route, you will have to actively promote your book. Lucky for you that's coming up next.

In the next chapter, I'm going to briefly talk about publicity, what it is, why you need it and the different ways to drum up publicity for your book.

Chapter 14

Getting publicity, everything you need to know to get your book known.

There's so many ways to get publicity for your book, your whole aim is to get a constant stream of people lining up outside your door, wanting to buy your book from you.

Can you just imagine how many copies of your book you will sell if your face or message was in at least one major media outlet a day?

This of course, is entirely possible. The media has the power to make you as rich and as famous as you want to be. All you need to do is know how to approach it correctly.

In this chapter I'm going to show you how to get all the publicity you could ever want. I'll be explaining how the media thinks and how they react to the press releases that come across their desk.

Now, like most things in life, there's a right way to do things and a wrong way. Luckily I learnt from the best, these are guys that have been journalists for magazines and huge media conglomerates.

You need to realise that publicity can be your ticket to fame and fortune, that's if you do it correctly. Lucky for you, I'm going to show you how to do it correctly. However, you need to understand this. It's no walk in the park. You have to be tenacious and work hard at it. It won't just fall into your lap. Rest assured, if you put the time and effort into creating a top-notch publicity campaign, you'll see the benefits for years to come.

What is publicity anyway?

Basically publicity is when you have something to say. You have some news, a point of view, or a product, like your book, and you'd like the media to get the message out to their listeners, readers, or viewers.

Now there's something you need to know about the media, unless you're ridiculously famous the media doesn't care about you or what you have to say. They care about themselves, their ratings, and getting as many people as they can tuning into their station or picking up their publication.

They do this by publicising things that they think, would interest their audience. It's your job to provide that stuff for them. It's a harmonious relationship, you provide them with the media they need, and they provide you with the publicity.

Why do so many get it wrong?

Before I go on and show you the tools, techniques and tactics I've learnt over the years, I want to have a chat about why so many people get it wrong.

Unfortunately publicity remains a puzzle to most people, they find themselves running to the library or downloading material from the Internet by so-called experts or "gurus." Then they'd spend countless hours going over the books and articles, most of which would tell them to get publicity you need to write a press release that explains who you are and what you're doing using the journalist 5 w's, (who, what, why, when and how.)

They'll tell you to wait a few days and then follow up with a response to see if they need any more information or need anymore help.

Unfortunately, those types of press releases are only used if the media is having a bad news day or if they can't think of anything else to put in their publication.

It's always sad to see individuals spending their hard earned cash on various books teaching these techniques only to find they get little or no media exposure and then give up trying to use publicity as an option for success.

Most people think that their publicity success is dependent on the whim of the media.

One of the most important things that you must remember, is no matter how highly we regard the media in society, they're just people like you and me. They've the same feelings, emotions and appeal to the same things as we do.

So if the population responds to something interesting, you can be sure that the media will find the same thing interesting. The only difference between the media and us is, the media has a keen sense of what interests the majority of people, whereas we only know what interests those who surround us.

Unfortunately, we think that the majority of people would be interested in us. Well, they're not, never have been and never will be, unless we give them a reason.

The Media Domino Effect or MDE.

When you give the media a reason to be interested in you, you open the floodgates to all the publicity you'll ever need.

And it's not going to be as expensive as you think, in fact the costs will be cheaper than you ever imagined. Would you believe me if I said to you, that you could get a full page in a trade publication, or a spot on the radio, or a column with your picture in a local newspaper for only a few pence?

Well that's all you will need initially, just a few pence to fax a press release. Nowadays, it's free, all you have to do is send an e-mail and that's it, you're done.

Once that's done you'll start to see the media domino effect or MDE come into play. For example, say you send a press release to a magazine and they decide to feature you in an article. The article is a success and is seen by a newspaper, they now want to do a piece on you, after that a TV station wants to book you as a guest and so it snowballs.

MDE means you can start out with something relatively small, like a spot on your local radio station and end up on a national TV show watched my millions.

MDE works well because if you're a good interviewer on the radio, you'll be good on TV and so on. If you were seen as an interesting character with something that would interest the reader, listeners or viewers, every producer would want you on their program. They'll be banging your door down to get an interview and promote your book.

Piggyback on current events.

The main aim of publicity is to get people into the bookstores or online to buy your book, or if you're selling it directly, to buy it from you and get more information.

One great way to do this is to piggyback the release of your book with something that is happening in the news. You can always guarantee that if something is trending in the news, the media would be interested in something similar.

So let's say your book is about the youth of today and how they react to their elders. You can piggyback your release with a news article on teen hoodlums terrorising the elderly. That may not be the greatest example but you get my point.

If you think creatively, you'll always be able to tie your book in with the current events.

Then there are the holidays and the seasons you can tie your book into. Along with the 4 seasons, you get the harvesting season, planting season, back to school season, etc. As for holidays, well more and more are springing up all the time. There's no end to the number of seasons and holidays you can tie the release of your book into.

Creating the winning headline

You can almost guarantee that every news bulletin that goes out, you will find a topic that you can tie in with your book.

Say you've written a book on successful tips for rapid weight-loss. You hear the news about the child obesity problem in Britain.

You know that your book can help thousands of children live a happier and healthier lifestyle if they follow your simple steps.

You immediately start working on your press release. It's absolutely essential that your headline is a grabber, it's essential to your success. The headline is the key. If you have a fantastic headline and a crappy media release, you'll still be in the running for success. If it's a crappy headline and great press release, you're dead in the water.

"Londoner has found the solution to eradicate child obesity in the UK."

I know what you may be thinking, is this truly possible? Has this person found a solution? Surely someone would've thought about it ages ago.

Maybe, however, if you were holding that headline in your hands, what would be forced to do? What would any curious human being be forced to do? Read the rest of the press release. You're intrigued to find out just what this solution is and how it can combat child obesity.

That's exactly what you want to do with the media, write a headline so compelling, it forces the reader to continue reading.

It's always wise to spend some time looking at powerful headlines. Dissecting them and finding out the elements that make them so successful. If you can copy that formula, you will have a lot of success.

The best place to find great headlines is the tabloids, yes they can be full of lies and nonsense, but they have perfected the art of writing irresistible headlines.

Find one that's not celebrity driven, rather headline driver. Essentially you're looking for the tabloids that get people reacting to the headlines rather than the people their profiling.

Forget about the who, what, where, when type of headlines, go for the ones like: "The eat anything you want to eat diet." Get the headlines that force you to read on.

Another place you can grab these headlines from is magazines, especially ones like Cosmopolitan, FHM or any other women's or men's magazine. These headlines or article headlines are designed to the potential buyer is literally forced to get the magazine so they can get the benefits of the articles.

Go to your library and try and get a few back issues to read and write down the article titles.

Creating the Press Release to follow the headline

Okay so you've written a sensational headline that will force the newsreader to carry on reading. Now you have to follow it up with the press release. Typically it's written on plain white paper, no need for logo's or letterheads.

In the top left hand corner, you must write the following choice of words: FOR IMMEDIATE RELEASE, FOR RELEASE ANYTIME ON OR AFTER (enter the date,) or FOR RELEASE ANYTIME ON OR BEFORE (enter the date.)

This will give the media a clear indication on when to send it out. For instance if your book has a Halloween theme you should write: FOR RELEASE ANYTIME ON OR BEFORE 31st OCTOBER.

Next on the top right hand corner, you should write: FOR FURTHER INFORMATION, CONTACT (enter your name and direct telephone number.)

Don't use the name of your company or organisation and make the phone number a direct line, perhaps an extension. Anything else and the media will dismiss the release for being too hard to follow up on.

Don't waste your precious time following up on a press release, if they haven't contacted you, the problem will be with the headline, re-write the headline and send it elsewhere.

After the headline comes the two-line explanation on what your story is all about. No matter how compelling, how intriguing, how many twists and turns your story has it can be boiled down to a two line explanation. Remember the headline above? Here's an example of the two-line explanation of that headline.

"Jane Huffman has discovered the secret to successful dieting and helps thousands to lose weight and keep it off."

After the two lines comes a brief explanation of the book in bullet points, like this.

•	Why Britain has become a nation of bingers and 3 easy steps to prevent it.

•	Five minute training techniques that can help keep the pounds off for good.

•	How eating the "right" fast foods can help you lose weight.

•	The 7 key elements you need in your diet that supercharges your metabolism.

And so on. If you do around ten points, the journalist will be banging your door down for an interview.

At the bottom of the first page, ensure you type in any media testimonials you may have that will add to your credibility.

The second page of your three-page press release is your biography. This is to show the media who you are, and why you'll make a good interview. All the information you write on this page should relate only to two things, you and your story. It's not a detailed description of your life or a resume. You aren't applying for a job. Before you write anything in your bio ask yourself what information has to do with the story and will the media be interested in the topic.

Include any previous writing accolades and include the reason why you'd be such an interesting guest.

The last page is where you'll include a Question sheet.

This is basically a sheet of paper with at least 20 questions you feel the media will be interested in asking if they interview you.

The media don't have time to research all the topics of the people they interview, if you give them a question sheet, even if they don't know a thing about the topic, they can be prepared simply by asking you the questions on the sheet you provided. What's more, you'll have the chance to study the questions, so you can plan the answers in advance and save yourself looking a fool on national television.

Always make sure a few of them are challenging, the media like this because it makes them look intelligent.

If you finally get a chance to be auditioned, never hold anything back. Tell them exactly what they want to know. You won't be giving out all the details in the book. You're simply giving out teasers so the audience will go out and buy your book.

Other forms of publicity

Every writer should, in essence, be a comfortable speaker. One of the best ways to publicise you book is to become a guest speaker at seminars. As you speak about your chosen topic, you're more than welcome to plug your new book.

Another one is to arrange book signings at your local library or bookshop. This couldn't be easier, just pop down to your local library or bookshop and tell them you are willing to do signings, you'll soon see a snowball effect as the surrounding bookshops and libraries hear about your success.

Using social media to sell your books
We're now living in an age where technological advances allow us to communicate over vast distances without ever having to leave the house. This can only be a good thing when it comes to getting publicity for your book.

Facebook recently passed 500,000,000 subscribers from all over the world, to ignore this for publicising your book would be a crime. If you haven't got a Facebook account yet, firstly, where have you been the last few years, secondly, you need to get one. It's completely free to sign up, just go **to www.facebook.com** and follow the easy steps.

From this point forward, I'm going to assume you have a Facebook account.

So plugging your new book couldn't be easier. You could write on your wall saying you have a new book coming out, make sure you tell your "friends" where you can get it from. Another way is setting up a fanpage of your book and invite your friends to join and then send messages via your fanpage.

Another great way to plug your book on Facebook is to find writing groups or groups that have the same interest in your topic. Join the group and then post messages on the group's wall.

One thing I should say though is, don't just plug your book, offer the audience a few chapters for free as a teaser, or occasionally add some value to your posts by giving away free valuable information. Your prospective customers will trust you a lot more if you give something away that's of value for free.

Other site you can use to plug your book is, if you haven't already heard of it, LinkedIn, found at **www.linkedin.com** or another one that is taking off at a rapid speed is Twitter, found at **www.twitter.com**. LinkedIn is a lot like Facebook but is more business orientated, while with twitter you can promote your book in the form of "tweets." **www.pinterest.com** is another social media site where you can plug your books through the use of various images, known as pins.

Whichever one you use, (I recommend using all 4,) social media is a fantastic platform to promote you and your book. By not using this type of media will drastically stunt your profits.

Other Online Publicity tricks

One way to drum up great publicity for you and your book is to join forums on writing and in the topic of your choice.

Many people look to forums for tips and advice on a whole host of topics. Your job will be to provide that advice and then plug your book in the signature bit.

Be careful though, always read the forums terms and conditions of what you can and can't post. Always respond to a few posts giving sound advice. People will soon see you're there to help. This makes you look trustworthy, so when it does come to plugging your book, it will make it far easier for your prospective client to buy from you.

In the chapter 15, I'm going to tell you why you should be writing your autobiography. Why it's imperative you write one and how it can be used as a marketing tool.

Chapter 15

The 10 facts of non-fiction writing and how this impacts writing an autobiography.

Before I show you exactly how to write an autobiography I thought I'd dedicate this very short chapter to the 10 facts of non-fiction writing, explaining the strengths and weaknesses of autobiographical writing.

Fact 1

Interesting people create interesting topics because they lead interesting lives.

While this may be true, don't let it discourage you from writing your autobiography. I say, let your love for writing help you to explore the world more and live the life to the fullest. The more different things you do, the more you can write about. Try and set yourself a challenge and do something new and exciting each month, then write about it. It doesn't have to be a book, just your thoughts on the experience in a diary of some sort. Life is full if interesting things to do go out and find adventure for yourself. I consider myself quite a boring person, however, my school life was far from boring. I went to boarding school in South Africa, and let me tell you it's not the posh boarding school you have in the U.K. It was hard, gritty and we got into all sorts of mischief. So while I think the rest of my life is pretty mundane, school certainly was not. So guess what my autobiography is mostly about?

Fact 2

Fact is stranger than fiction, however, creative lying is more interesting than both, and quite often greater truth is found in a lie.

Non-fiction writers always assume they need to tell the truth, the whole truth and nothing but the truth. However, sometimes a lie can tell a greater truth than actual truth can. I know this sounds ridiculous, but let me explain. Say you're writing an historical autobiography and you start by saying, "It happened around..." This is the worst thing you can say because not knowing the exact date makes you instantly lose credibility in all the other facts of the experience. When you've admitted that you can't remember certain dates, you cause the reader to doubt the soundness of your memory. So instead, to gain the trust of your readers, even though you don't know the exact date, rather start by saying something like, "It happened on March the 4th at 11pm."

Fact 3

Don't be too close to your subject when you attempt to write about it, strong emotions just hamper your writing.
The day I met my wife, was one of the best days of my life. However, that night, when I wanted to write about my experience, my emotions and what I was feeling was so strong, I just couldn't put it into words. This is a natural occurrence that happens to everyone. The best thing you can do is wait a while for your emotions to settle before writing about the event.

As a rule of thumb, if you have a powerfully negative experience, wait 2 years to write about it. If it was a profoundly positive experience, wait 1 year. The reason for this is, you remember negative experiences a lot longer than positive ones.

Fact 4

Really good life stories should either have a positive message or at least end in a positive way.
Studies have found that the human brain can process 55,000 thoughts a day. 79% of those are negative. If you want to stand out from the crowd, try writing about your positive experiences. It's fine to put a few negative experiences in, that's how you were moulded from the person you are today. But for the sake of the reader, try to make your book as positive as possible.

I remember reading an autobiography of a friend of mine, part of the story was about his mother's battle with cancer, although this was very sad, it had a good ending, he met the love of his life at the hospital his mother went to. Going back to my school days, a lot of bullying went on and for the most part, my experiences were bad, however, I'm not dwelling on the bad things, rather, I'm concentrating on the funny things that happened, with a few sprinkles of the bad scattered in between the chapters.

We see news reports of negative things that happen every day. So it's always refreshing to read about something positive for a change.

Fact 5

The best life stories are written in first person and present tense in order to capture the excitement of the moment.
While this may need a little creativity on your part, it's always a better read when read in first person and present tense. First of all, you'll find that when you pretend, almost if you've created a time machine that allows you to live the past, you'll double your memory comprehension. Details you thought were lost in the recesses of you mind, will quickly swim to the forefront.

By writing in present tense, you also breathe life into the characters that have long since passed away. When you write about them in the present as if they were alive, they continue to remain alive as long as your written word survives.

One of the biggest benefits to the reader when writing in present tense is that feel that they are not reading about history, instead it's like they're experiencing the moment with you there and then.

Fact 6

An autobiography is always interesting if it has several characters in it, even if all those characters were you.
Sounds strange I know, but ask yourself this question. Were you the same person you were 10 years ago, or even 5 years ago?

I bet you the answer is a resounding no. Life changes and people change too. My personality now is very different to the personality I had in school.

A major downfall of some autobiographies is when the writer describes himself as the person they are today, throughout all the stages of his life.

At the very least, give yourself a different character for every 5 years you've been on this planet, that way the story will capture the evolution of your personality and will be a more interesting read.

Fact 7

The true testament to an amateur autobiography is when the author writes his life in chronological order.

This is one of the things editors look for to see if it was written by an un-creative person or not.

The easiest way to avoid this is by changing the order of the body. You can write the start as the start of your life and the end as the most current and up to date person you are, however, in order to not be seen as an amateur, you need to swap the body around a bit and this is how you do it.

Divide the body of your story into three sections. Then look at each section and decide what portion is the most interesting, what's the second most interesting and what's the least interesting. Now all you have to do is shuffle them around and write them in this order: 1, then 3, then 2.

The most interesting must be told first, the least interesting told second and the second most interesting told third.

The reason for this is first to hook your reader with the most exciting part, this will force them to read on, then you have the least interesting, which is still quite interesting anyway, this will coast them through to the second most interesting, which ends the story with a bang, so it's sort of a roller-coaster ride for the reader.

You'll have some creative thinking to do, but if you get this right, it will add fascination to the story.

Fact 8

The mistakes you're reluctant to tell the reader are things the reader wants to read the most.

Normally it's those stories that the reader benefits the most from. Humans normally learn better from the mistakes they've made than from their successes. If you're successful, you savour that success. However, if you fail, you want to analyse your mistake to prevent it from happening again. So, if you don't tell your readers about your failures, you'll be denying them the wisdom of your experience.

Admitting to your weaknesses also adds to your credibility. It makes you human in the reader's eyes. If you throw in a few failures, it helps the reader to believe your successes.

People can't relate to supermen, they only relate to human beings, so when you admit your greatest weakness or failure, the reader's admire you and think, "I'm glad I'm not the only one who made that mistake."

By admitting your mistakes, you'll get the reader to identify, sympathise, empathise and laugh with you.

Fact 9

Good Life stories have a message for the reader.
The author has learned from his experience and now has passed his knowledge on. However, it's the reader choice on whether they should follow and apply that knowledge to their own lives. If you have experienced something deeply enough, you should've learnt something from it. For this reason, the wisdom found in an autobiography always exceeds the wisdom found in fiction.

Fact 10

The more years your experience took place, the better your story.
The problem when writing a true life story when the information is fresh, the writer tends to waffle on a bit about it. As time passes, it's not the negative or positive things that you forget first, it's the boring insignificant details, the details that have no place in the story.

The loss of the boring details greatly improves a life story, and the important bits always come back to you as you write them.

When done right, out of all the genres out there in the world and autobiography makes the best reading.

In the next chapter we are going to talk about the different techniques, both paid and free, on how to get your book written for you. Keep reading, this is going to be an exciting one.

Chapter 16

The Lazy way to write. How to get other people to write books for you.

By now you should have learnt nearly every tool I have in my arsenal that will allow you to write your book faster than you ever thought possible. Right? If you haven't, I suggest going back and re-reading this book to get a firm understanding of the strategies and techniques.

However, even after all this training I've provided, you still might think you don't have time to write a book. Well, you know what I think about that, but hey, I'm not here to judge. Then again, you may not want to write your book but rather have someone else write it for you.

Well in this chapter, I'm going to discuss the various ways of getting other people to write your book for you. Now some of the methods you have to pay for, however, I have a strategy that if you're on a tight budget, you're going to love, because you won't have to pay a penny to get your book written for you.

Hiring a Ghostwriter to write your book for you.

So what is a ghostwriter anyway? Well, it's not some apparition, presence or deity you pray to that comes in the middle of the night and writes your book for you, pfft, that's just silly.

A ghostwriter is someone you hire, that will take your ideas and write the book for you, under your name. A lot of celebrities have their autobiographies written this way. In most cases the ghostwriter doesn't even get credited for writing the book.

Now there's a plethora of places you can find ghostwriters that are willing to do your work for you. Search engines like **Google.com, Yahoo.com** and **Bing.com** will spit out a load of websites offering this service. However, the sites I like to use, when I want articles created for me are either **Freelancer.com** or **Elance.com**. These sites have a great reputation when it comes to quality.

All you need to do is sign up for an account and post a job on either site stating exactly what you're looking for. Soon you'll see members putting in bids. What I would highly recommend is firstly, read the feedback or comments from previous users that have used your ghostwriters' service in the past. Then you want to ask them for a sample of their work. Don't be afraid to ask them to write a quick article of a subject of your choosing. If I were to do it, I would ask them to write an article on the topic of my book. You'll be doing this because you want to see if their writing is acceptable. If they refuse, simply move on to the next person. Now most of the users will have their hourly rate, I believe you can always haggle the price down, so don't be afraid to do so.

Another site you can use, but I haven't, is **ODesk.com**. They work in the same principal as Elance and Freelancer, whereas you tell them what you want and they put in a bid for the work.

One thing I would like to mention is though; don't always go for the cheapest quote. I constantly hear of complaints that the person someone hired was relatively cheap, but their work was less than sub-standard. However, like I mentioned previously, get them to give you a sample of their work so you can judge the quality yourself.

Use your research to your advantage

Now here's a pretty cool strategy that you could use, which combines the research aspect and getting your book written for you.

Okay, if you remember, we spoke about getting an expert to interview for research purposes. Right?

Firstly, there will be a little writing to do on your part, and that is the outline and blueprint. So, you know what you want your book to be about, and you have the 15 questions for each chapter. The next part is to find a group of experts to interview. Have the questions you want answers to (the blueprint) close at hand and make sure you can record the interview. You can use Skype or some other conferencing software for this.

Now approach the expert like I told you in the research part of this book. Tell them you aren't an expert (even if you are,) and you would love to interview them on their chosen topic, as you are writing a book on the subject and you would love to hear their opinion. Basically you want to stroke their ego to make it impossible for them to say no.

Tell them it won't take more than ten minutes or so. Once they say yes, have your 15 questions to hand, press record, and conduct the interview.

It's entirely up to you, but you could ask just one expert all the questions or distribute the questions between experts. Personally, I would ask one expert for each chapter, you don't want to scare them away with hundreds of questions. Fifteen questions isn't too long or too short, if fact it's just right. (Like the Goldilocks reference I just threw in there.)

Once you have all the questions answered, you have a book. The only thing you need to do now, is either pay someone to transcribe the book for you, or you could do it yourself.

The great advantage of this method is you could have all the questions written out, answered and transcribed in a matter of days.

One word of caution when it comes to this method though, you need to inform the expert that you intend to use the interview in your book and ask for their permission to do so.

I know of a fellow that used this method and went on to become a bestseller. However, he didn't ask the experts permission to use the interview in the book and got sued. So always make sure you have the experts permission, this eliminates any nasty surprises in the future.

Getting a group of people to write your book for free.

This method works extremely well for both fiction and non-fiction.

There's various ways to approach and utilise this method. Let's look at non-fiction first. Firstly, you need to find a group of writers that you already know have written either a book, or article on your chosen niche or topic. You can do this by searching on Amazon or Google. Let's say for instance you want to write a book on how to get traffic to your website. As you know there are a variety of techniques you can use to generate traffic. Like paid traffic, using Google or Facebook ads, there's article marketing, link building, video marketing, SEO, etc, etc.

All you need to do is find a group of people that specialise in each area. Once you have a list of ten or so people, it's time to contact them. Tell them you are thinking about writing a book on their topic and you would love to have them contribute to the book. You may have to do some serious schmoozing to get them to do it for free. You could say that you are willing to promote their other books or services or help them in other ways.

Alternatively, you could say that you will give them a percentage of the profits, or a percentage of the profits will be going to charity. However, if you say you are going to give a percentage to charity, make sure you do so; you don't want to give yourself a bad reputation and ruin your credibility. These authors could help you write another book, so you don't want to burn any bridges. Once you have them on board, ask them if they can write an article on their chosen expertise. Each article will be a chapter for your book. If you have ten writers each contributing a chapter, you'll have ten chapters, on the various ways to drive traffic to your site, which is more than enough. Your job will be to bring it all together with some savvy editing and then getting it into print or online.

Fiction writing is pretty much the same. Find a group of writers that write in the genre you want to write. Again, you can find them on Google, Amazon, writing forums, Facebook groups, etc. Tell them you want to write a book and you are looking for contributors to help.

Some of them may say no, but there are a whole lot of writers out there that just write for the recognition. There's two ways they can do this. One, they can write a chapter each.

The problem here is each would have to read what the other has written, so they can continue where the other left off, in order for it to flow smoothly. If you don't do this, you run the risk of the book being a bunch of disjointed thoughts that won't be fun for anyone to read.

Alternatively, you could ask each of them to present their own individual short story. This way all you need to do is combine them all into one neat little book. I know of a few writers that have done this successfully in the past.

Once you have found enough writers that are willing to help you, tell them what you require or possibly even get them on Google Hangout and discuss the project between each other.

Then, as you get the work back, it will be up to you to edit then work, and get it to print.

What I love about this method is it's very interactive; you could have a lot of fun with this and in the end make a whole new group of friends with the same interests as you.

There you have it, three simple, yet effective ways to get your book written for you. Some of the techniques will cost you a bit, however, some, with a little bit of forward thinking and persuasion could cost you nothing.

In the final chapter we are going to talk a little more about writing your life story, why you should write it, how's it's a great tool to have in your marketing arsenal and the questions you need to ask yourself to make writing your autobiography child's play.

<u>Chapter 17</u>

Writing your Autobiography, why everyone should write one, why it's one of the greatest marketing tools in your arsenal and the questions you need to ask yourself in order to write it.

Writing a life story isn't just about you telling your audience about the life you lived, the mistakes you've made, how you rectified them, and your successes. It also tells the audience how you became that person you are today. What lessons in life did you learn and how they too, can achieve the success you've had, if they follow in your footsteps. An autobiography is one big testimonial of your life. It gets the reader to relate to you, to know you better. It's to gain your audiences trust. If a reader reads your autobiography and likes it, the next time they see one of your products on the shelf, they're more likely to buy it because they instantly recognise you and have an unfaltering trust in you.

Another reason why you should write an autobiography is because you will be leaving a legacy behind. It's sad to see in life that very few people know who their ancestors were, never mind the life they lived, or what achievements or accomplishments they made.

Let me ask you a question. Do know any of the names or your great grand parents? I bet you that it's something you can't even remember because you haven't been told. What makes it sadder is that, that information is lost. Yet, your great grandparents lived their lives on this earth not more than 100 years ago.

Now let me ask you another question. A 100 years from now, who's going to remember your name? 100 years from now, people won't remember what it felt like the first time you fell in love, how you liked to sing you're daughter to sleep or that you were the first person in your class to graduate with honours. You'll only be remembered by the words that you put down on paper.

Wouldn't it be nice if you could read a book that told you how your great grandparents lived, what mischief they got up to in their teens and if they had a similar personality to yourself? It's just not possible, what is possible though is you can write your life story right now, so that your great grand children can read all about what happened to you, way back in 2013.

Now I've already taught you the writing strategy to get a book written faster than you thought possible. Now I'm going to show you how you can write your life story in mere hours!

Have you ever found yourself bored with nothing to do? Almost everyone has. What about when you have a few hours spare, when you've nothing better to do.

Well if you have these spare moments, instead of staring at TV you don't really want to watch, why don't you start the process of writing your life story.

You can start by asking yourself, and writing down, some basic questions. Questions about things that happened in your life, you need to make them very specific and avoid being general.

Questions like: Describe how you felt the first time you kissed someone? Why is red your favourite colour? When you were 8 years old, what made you crash your bike you got for Christmas? What was the house you lived in, in your teens, look like?

Create between 200 to 300 questions, making them specific.

As soon as you've done that, go back to the first question, read it and then close your eyes. Let your memory take you back and visualise the answer to the question. Put yourself in the picture as if you were standing right there. Try to remember how you felt at that specific point in time, what do your senses tell you? Now write down three words that will best describe your answer.

Do that for all the questions.

By now you should be quite familiar with the technique, but for those that need reminding here goes...

Get out your timer, and you guessed it, add 5 minutes to the countdown. Pick any question you want to answer first. It doesn't have to be number 1. Start with one of the three words, the other two need to be in the first paragraph. Begin the timer and write as fast as you can for the five minutes until the timer goes off. Finish after the timer stops and go to the next question.

If you have 300 questions, it should take you about 25 hours to write.

Now if you think that thinking of 300 questions is too hard, let me give you a head start. I've provided you with 150 questions. Use them if you like, or create your own.

1.) Where were you born?

2.) Who were your parents?

3.) When you was a kid, were you ever frightened of anything?

4.) Was there any childhood trauma in your life?

5.) Who was the strictest out of your parents?

6.) When you were a child, if you happened to look out your bedroom window, what did you see?

7.) What was the first pet you owned and what did you call it?

8.) Who was your childhood best friend and how did you meet?

9.) What was the best thing about having your pet?

10.) When was the first time you got into serious trouble?

11.) Where did you attend primary school?

12.) Who was the first person you kissed and what did it feel like?

13.) Is there anything interesting that ever happened in primary school?

14.) What was your first major achievement in life?

15.) Did you have a favourite bed-time story, if so, what was it?

16.) What's your favourite colour and how has it affected your life?

17.) What was the best thing about your childhood friend?

18.) Were you ever affected by the death of a family member early on in life? If so, how did it change you?

19.) What was your favourite music as a child?

20.) What was the most embarrassing thing to happen to you as a child?

21.) Explain how you felt when you hit puberty.

22.) Who was your first serious girlfriend?

23.) How'd you feel when you broke up?

24.) Did you ever try to get into a club when you were underage?

25.) When did you first get drunk?

26.) Who did you look up to when you were young?

27.) Who taught you to tie your shoelaces?

28.) How'd you learn to ride a bike?

29.) How'd you learn to swim?

30.) What was your most embarrassing moment as a teenager?

31.) What was your favourite game as a child?

32.) What did you do during the school holidays?

33.) Who was your favourite teacher at school and why were they so good?

34.) What's your greatest accomplishment?

35.) What was your worst romantic date?

36.) When was the first time you had intercourse and how did it feel?

37.) Were you ever in a bad accident?

38.) What's the best Christmas present you've been given?

39.) What was your first major holiday?

40.) Have you gone anywhere exotic?

41.) Did you ever do poorly in certain subjects at school?

42.) What's been your biggest disappointment?

43.) What's your biggest regret in life?

44.) What's the saddest day you can remember?

45.) What's the happiest day you can remember?

46.) What was the first party you went to?

47.) What's the best party you've ever been to?

49.) What happened when you went camping for the first time?

50.) Do you believe in karma?

51.) How has religion moulded your life?

52.) Have you ever thought of starting your own business?

53.) What did you want to be when you grew up?

54.) Who taught you to read?

55.) How did you meet the love of your life?

56.) What's the most romantic thing you've done?

57.) What do you think about technology?

58.) What's been your favourite job and why?

59.) What's the one place you would really like to go and why?

60.) Do you like to cook?

61.) What's your favourite movie and why?

62.) What's your favourite book and why?

63.) What do you like to do in your spare time?

64.) What's the best lesson you learnt for either of your parents?

65.) Who taught you to drive?

66.) Have you ever wanted to learn to play and instrument?

67.) Have you ever been charitable?

68.) Who in life do you respect the most?

69.) What are you good at?

70.) Have you ever been beaten up and what happened?

71.) Is your life the way you wanted it to be?

72.) Have you ever learnt to ride a motorbike?

73.) Have you ever ridden a horse?

74.) What's the most daring thing you've ever done?

75.) What was your favourite fairy tale as a child?

76.) Have you ever had a serious medical problem?

77.) Have you ever had a near death experience?

78.) Has something ever happened to you that you can't explain?

79.) What's the biggest mistake you've ever made?

80.) What kind of furniture do you like?

81.) If you were a super hero, what would your abilities be?

82.) Who is your best friend now?

83.) Have you ever felt that you should've been born in another time?

84.) Do you believe in life after death?

85.) Do you believe in other life in the universe?

86.) To whom have you given the most of yourself to?

87.) Describe the first bike you ever had?

88.) What's the most meaningful gift you've ever received?

89.) What's your biggest lie?

90.) What's the worst thing anyone has ever said to you?

91.) If you were trapped on a desert island with only three books, what will they be?

92.) What's the most fun form or transport you've been on?

93.) How did you feel the first time you went on a roller coaster?

94.) What would you think people would say when you die?

95.) When you see a picture of earth from space, what do you feel?

96.) Have you ever wanted to be an actor, rock star or someone famous?

97.) Think of the last person you knew that died. What did they teach you about life?

98.) Who has had the most profound effect on you in life?

99.) Describe your route to school when you were a kid?

100.) Were you ever bullied and did you ever get back at them?

101.) If you could have one personality attribute that you don't have, what would it be?

102.) What causes you to be so shy?

103.) Who's given you the most unusual gift?

104.) What's your favourite hobby?

105.) How do people react when you talk about your hobby?

106.) What skill that you have developed has been the most important to you?

107.) What do you think about when you see fireworks?

108.) What was your most special birthday?

109.) What was it like stepping into your first home you owned?

110.) What's the biggest challenge in getting old?

111.) Have you ever played an April Fool's joke?

112.) Are you superstitious and how does it affect you?

113.) What's your feeling on business?

114.) What's your favourite food?

115.) What's the worst attribute a person can have?

116.) Are you an organised person?

117.) Describe the first place you lived in after leaving your parents house?

118.) Are you afraid of dying and what do you think will happen after you die?

119.) What depresses you?

120.) When were you in your last fight?

121.) What's the most unusual bed you've slept in?

122.) What's the most challenging thing you do in life?

123.) Do you have any unfulfilled dreams?

124.) Can you think of a party that was a complete disaster?

125.) What's your favourite sport and why?

126.) Why do you dress the way you do?

127.) Think back to the first time you drove in the rain, how did you feel and what did you see?

128.) What has your longest walk been and how did it happen?

129.) Some people find fault with your level of ambition, Why do you think this is?

130.) What was the first job you ever had?

131.) What's been the most important contribution to your community?

132.) Why do you think it's important to write your life story?

133.) Do you have a favourite plant?

134.) What's your favourite flower?

135.) What's the most embarrassing thing that's happened in a wedding you attended?

136.) Describe your personality when you were 18.

137.) Have you ever been athletic?

138.) What's your view on politics?

139.) What's the most spectacular piece of scenery you've ever seen?

140.) What makes you laugh?

141.) Have you ever been self employed?

142.) Do you believe in God?

143.) Have you ever had a traumatic experience growing up?

144.) What's the most immoral thing you've ever done?

145.) Did your parents ever catch you doing something naughty?

146.) What's your favourite game?

147.) If you could script your last words, what would they be?

148.) What song would you want playing at your funeral?

149.) What's the funniest thing ever to happen to you?

150.) What is your doctor like?

I hope you now have enough to start your life story, you should easily think of another 150 questions on your own.

Well, there you have it. You now have all the tools and knowledge to write a book in under a month. Read through the chapters thoroughly until you have grasped the concepts and they become second nature to you.

I hope you've benefitted from this book and I look forward to hearing all your successes.

Now go! **Start writing your book!**

<u>Conclusion</u>

Well that's it. I hope you have learnt a lot in this course, have started to implement the techniques and strategies, and are well on your way to becoming a successful published author. You, my fellow author, are the future of writing; your words are just begging to be read. Just make sure it's a bloody good book that the readers will enjoy and they will most certainly reward your efforts by firstly, becoming a raving fan, eager to buy your next book, and then your marketer by spreading the word.

Please use all the resources available to you and remember, if you need any help whatsoever, please contact me via e-mail.

If you have enjoyed reading this book, please take a few minutes of your time to write a review and publish it wherever you got it from. Also it would be nice if you could tell your friends and colleagues to go and get it. Your help by spreading the word would be much appreciated.

Good Luck and I wish you all the success you deserve.

Happy Writing and Publishing my friend!

Regards,

Glen Palmer

****

<u>About The Author</u>

Glen Palmer is the creator of **frompen2print.com & glen-palmer.com.** He lives in Barnsley – UK with my wife Marie-Clare and English Springer Spaniel Shaggy. He's been involved with various writing workshops, teaching the techniques and strategies you've learnt in this very course.

He's been writing – well – ever since he could hold a pen really. He's always been interested in storytelling, clearly remembering the times he was kid when he sat around campfires telling his friends stories. He noticed from a very early age that he had a very active imagination, so decided to give writing a try.

He had a pretty boring upbringing in South Africa; however, He's always been interested in writing. He was editor of my school paper and enjoyed writing poems and short stories in a little black book. He completed high school with relatively good grades and attended university, studying Criminal Psychology. Unfortunately, his life didn't turn out as he'd planned it, and due to lack of funds, he had to quit university. From there he drifted from job to job not really knowing what he wanted. It was only when he returned to England in May 1999 that he decided to reignite my passion and give writing a go.

Before he actually wrote my first novel, he realised he needed a little help and direction, so he did a few years of intense work on studying writing techniques, character and plot development and many other strategies. Contained within this manual, is a culmination of all those techniques and strategies, which you now, have the chance to study and master.

Glen truly believes you don't need any super skills or years studying Creative Writing at University to be able to write a book, whether it's fiction or non-fiction. In fact, the only reason he brought a load of courses on the subject was because I absolutely LOVE writing. It's in his blood, and it's his passion. Another of his passions is helping people with their writing, which is why he wrote this book. Now all you need to become a successful writer is this course. Devour the knowledge contained within these pages and implement what is taught.

The only way you'll fail is if you don't implement the techniques. He urges you to write every day, even if it's just a couple of lines. The more you write, the easier it will become and you'll soon see that writing can be a lot of fun indeed.

If you take any advise from this book it will be this – **write every day!**

Coming Soon:

If you enjoyed reading Super Simple Strategies To Write Any Book For Profit In 30 Days or Less, then you may also enjoy:

Simple Writing Strategies Presents: How To Write A Profitable Non-Fiction Book In Under 50 Hours.

Connect With Glen Palmer.

Blog: **http://glen-palmer.com**

Twitter: **https://twitter.com/GlenPInvest**

Facebook **https://www.facebook.com/glen.palmer.752**

LinkedIn: **http://www.linkedin.com/profile/view?id=85589219**

Google+: **https://plus.google.com/u/0/102008672182417524567**

<u>Resources</u>

Now that you have all the weapons in your arsenal to write a book in under a month, I've decided to go one step further. While this wouldn't be the route I would go down myself, it's only fair I give you the best possible start to your writing career. So below you'll find a successful agent acquisition letter and a synopsis highlight. Use this as a template for your own letter. I have also dissected it, showing you exactly why it's so popular. Along with the letter, you'll also find a few other recourses I've accumulated over my writing career.

This letter was written by one of my mentors and was hugely successful. So much so he had his pick of agents to choose from. In a moment, I'll show you why it was so successful. But first, let's start with the letter.

28th October, 2011

Thomas Brady

123 Park Road

London

N1 2FG

Dear Mr Brady:

Earn A College Degree in Four Months or Less is more than just a dream. It is a book I have just finished that is guaranteed to spread across the country like wildfire.

In case you're concerned that the title sounds "too good to be true," know that I've actually been conservative in my claim. In reality, it's possible to earn a fully accredited Bachelor's degree from scratch in less than TWO months!

I know, I received my own regionally accredited degree this way and have fully investigated all the best educational shortcuts for three years.

Being a former editor, I am well aware of the necessity of brevity, therefore this letter is purposefully short. Included with it is a synopsis, which "highlights" just a few of the best-kept educational secrets, revealed in this book:

The reason I use the term "popular" is because I am very active on the lecture circuit.

At just one well-attended lecture alone, just mentioning the book title caused more than a fifty percent buy rate...and this was for a product that was "sight unseen." It hadn't even been finished yet! Not only that, but this is the only book I've written where people continually ask if they can have extra brochures for their friends!

The economy is ripe for this book...and will be for many years to come. The job market has never been so competitive than it is now. People need to earn a college degree in order to compete. This book allows them to do so in a hurry.

I found your name listed as an agent with experience in "how-to" books. If you like to represent my finished and polished book, please notify me as soon as possible. I'm looking for a qualified agent to work with right now...for this book and several others that are soon to follow.

All the best,

XXXX

Now let's have a look at why this letter was dynamite and a letter the agents couldn't resist reading.

But before I do that, note the length of the letter, only 1 page. Agents are very busy people indeed, each day they have to sift through a mountain of acquisition letters. The longer the proposal is, the longer it takes them to read it. If they see it's more than 1 page, it normally gets put in the rejection pile before they've even had a chance to read it. So it's in your best interest to keep your letter to 1 page, if you want it read.

Earn A College Degree in Four Months or Less is more than just a dream. It is a book I have just finished that is guaranteed to spread across the country like wildfire.

The letter immediately told the agent what the book was about, and did so in such a way to pique the curiosity of the agent, forcing him to read on.

In case you're concerned that the title sounds "too good to be true," know that I've actually been conservative in my claim. In reality, it's possible to earn a fully accredited Bachelor's degree from scratch in less than TWO months!

Because the subject of the book was "hard to believe", he needed to legitimise the subject. Again this was done in such a way that it boosted the agent's initial curiosity.

I know, I received my own regionally accredited degree this way and have fully investigated all the best educational shortcuts for three years.

It's vitally important to let the agent know the depth of your experience on the subject. The more you sound like an expert, the greater the chances of acceptance. In this case the author let them know he had extensive personal experience and had researched it well.

Being a former editor, I am well aware of the necessity of brevity, therefore this letter is purposefully short. Included with it is a synopsis, which "highlights" just a few of the best-kept educational secrets, revealed in this book:

It is one thing to be an expert, but quite another to write about it. After grabbing the agent's attention by letting him know the author was the right person to write the book, he immediately found a way of mentioning his professional expertise in the writing field.

The reason I use the term "popular" is because I am very active on the lecture circuit. At just one well-attended lecture alone, just mentioning the book title caused more than a fifty percent buy rate...and this was for a product that was "sight unseen." It hadn't even been finished yet! Not only that, but this is the only book I've written where people continually ask if they can have extra brochures for their friends!

This is where the author shows the books marketability, so the agent can get excited about the sale potential. That's the whole reason they're in the business, to make money.

The economy is ripe for this book...and will be for many years to come. The job market has never been so competitive than it is now. People need to earn a college degree in order to compete. This book allows them to do so in a hurry.

It's important to mention the books marketability, but it's just as important to mention that it's not all about the money. You will want to convince the agent that the world needs your book.

I found your name listed as an agent with experience in "how-to" books. If you like to represent my finished and polished book, please notify me as soon as possible. I'm looking for a qualified agent to work with right now...for this book and several others that are soon to follow.

This was the most carefully thought-out paragraph of all. It starts off by letting the agent know he didn't just pick the agent's name out of a hat. He let the agent know he shopped around and chose him specifically because their expertise was in the same field as the authors. This also lets the agent know that the author is a professional and not any agent will do, he wants the best.

Also notice the words "finished" and "polished" book. He went out of his way to mention that he's not a "would-be author". He's a writer with a finished product ready to be sold.

The vast majority of letters agents receive are from unpublished writers who haven't yet completed their first book. Agents also know that out of that majority, only a handful will actually complete their book. So if you are a first-time writer, I would suggest you complete your book before submitting to an agent, you'll have a much higher chance of acceptance by doing this.

Also note that he didn't just say it was finished. Agents also know that the majority of first time writers finished book still needs a lot of work done to it before it becomes publishable. That's why he went out of his way and said it was "polished".

A time limit was placed in the last paragraph when he said he was looking for an agent right "now," he also insinuated they must have the proper qualifications. By telling the agent he was "looking," let them know as subtly as possible that if they were interested, they'd better jump on board quick, because he'd contacted other agents as well.

That statement alone resulted in him receiving his first yes in only 6 days after mass mailing. The second came a week later.

Lastly, he ended the letter by saying, **"this book and several others that are soon to follow."** What first-time writers don't realise is that around 60% of all published books don't make a red cent for the publisher. This means the agent doesn't make a lot either. So if the agent knew you only had one book, the agent would know that he only had around a 40% chance of make a little money off it. Even if you said you would be writing another, the agent would still have less than a 100% chance of making much money off the second book. However, in the author's case, he'd already mentioned he had one book, but also mentioned future "books," which according to the odds, would give the agent at least a 120% of making money from the author. For a smart agent, those odds would be too good to let slip away.

The synopsis

Earn A College Degree in Four Months or Less!

Synopsis of highlights

- Earn a Bachelor's degree in four months without taking a single course.

- Where to get a Four-year degree for less than $1000.

- Accredited Universities that award a degree based on life experiences.

- How to qualify with no maths course or exam.

- Earn 120 units of credit including 60 upper division for only $196.

- Special tips for bankers, insurance workers, and federal employees.

- How to earn an instant "major" by taking a 3-hour test.

- The university that gives you unlimited life experience credits for $30.

- Legitimate schools where you design your own degree.

- Receive credit for every old course no matter how long ago.

- Where to buy all your homework and term papers.

- Where you can get your educational needs assessed for as little as $15.

- What corporation and government training programs are worth credit.

- Hot to find out how many credits your military experience is worth.

- Five tests a person can take to be awarded a Bachelor's degree.

- Receive 18 semester credits for being fluent in another language.

- Receive a full year's worth of credit for doing a 3-hour test.

- Why attending four years of school is one of life's biggest rip-offs.

- How to earn three years of your degree at a community college.

- How to earn a degree by challenging final exams.

- Receive $72,000 in financial aid whether you have low income or not.

- Where to find consultants to give you free educational advise.

  And much, much more...

As you can see the author has highlighted all the benefits the reader will gain from reading this book. It shows the agent practically everything there is in the book as bullet points. You're aim when writing the synopsis is to do the same. If you list all the benefits in the synopsis, you're showing the agent that you know what you're talking about and exactly how it's going to benefit the reader, thus making the decision to take you on as a client a much easier one.

Best of luck on your publishing prowess.

Writing Resources

The Writer's Handbook

This is a book that comes out annually. It has a list of agent's names and addresses, with the genre they specialise in from all over the world.

It's available from most good bookstores as well as online sites like Amazon.

The Writer's and Artist's Yearbook

This is another book that comes out annually. It has the same info in this book as the writer's handbook.

Again, this is available from most good bookstores and online.

http://www.firstwriter.com

If you prefer finding publishers and agents online, then this is the site for you. For a minimal subscription fee, you can get all the names and addresses for publishers and agents all over the world. It also shows you magazine submissions if you are into writing short stories as well as a list of current writing competitions.

http://www.enhancemywriting.com

Quoted straight from their site: "You'll find everything on and off the Net that you could possibly need in writing or researching a paper, including links to all sorts of reference material, links to writing labs, links to Web search engines, and links to writing-related Web sites."

http://www.dictionary.com

Self explanatory really.

http://www.thesaurus.com

Same as above.

http://www.internet-resources.com

Here you'll find links to any sort of research your heart desires. I use this quite a lot when doing research for various articles and short stories.

http://www.writingresources.com

Quoted from their site: "This is a one-stop online resource site for both aspiring and professional writers, journalists and editors. We aim to provide you with useful information, writing tips, tutorials for beginners, and even news in the field of writing."

Interviewing experts for research and getting publicity

http://www.expertclick.com

This site is fantastic for finding an expert in your field to interview. I highly recommend you take a look at this site.

http://www.rtir.com

Rtir basically stands for Radio TV Interview report, it's a site that allows you to interview experts for research and it also allows you to sign up to get interviewed, so it can work both ways, get the research and the publicity you want. What more can you ask for.

http://www.liveperson.com

Again this can work two-fold. Here's what they have to say about themselves: "At LivePerson, our mission is to create lasting, meaningful connections. This inspires us to serve our customers exceptionally, to work together efficiently, and to get personally involved in our local communities. Our emphasis on connection leads to more opportunity— whether it's increased value for our customers, product innovation, or community growth. Our platform helps our customers engage with consumers in a way that strengthens brand loyalty and generates lifetime value for their business. Connection at the workplace inspires a deeper level of trust and appreciation in our team, helping us work together to achieve the next level of success and innovation."

http://www.ehow.com

Want to know how something works, how to build anything or ask practically any question known to man? Well then this is the site for you. It's got tons of info on anything and everything. It's a fantastic resource tool.

Writing Forums for research and publicity

http://www.writersbeat.com

The official writing forums of Writer's Beat. Post your stories, share some feedback, read the e-zine, become part of the writing community!

http://www.legendfire.com

LegendFire is a free, author-driven, online creative writing community. Our purpose is to provide a place where authors and poets of a broad range of genres can go to exchange feedback, make friends, and have fun!

http://www.writingforums.com

Writing Forums is a friendly, active literary community where you can talk with other writers, get feedback on your work, discuss ideas, share tips & tricks, network with others and lots more

http://www.writingforums.org

A writing forum, dedicated to creative writing, where writers can use writing workshops, share techniques, and discuss every aspect of writing, publishing, and marketing.

http://www.thenextbigwriter.com

A writing forum where writers can come together to discuss their writing, receive helpful writing tips and advice

Top 10 Self-Publishers.

1.) Palmer Publishing

http://www.frompen2print.com

This is a self-publishing service I offer, with extremely competitive prices. I personally work one to one with all my clients making sure they get the best professional service money can buy. I also work closely with my Graphic Designers, Editors, and the publishing team that have a combined publishing experience of over 100 years. The services available are: Personal, Starter, Intermediate, Professional Publishing, e-book service and cover design. Prices start from £99.

2.) Lulu

http://www.lulu.com

The Lulu Professional Services team is equipped with an array of first class editors, designers, writers and marketers with experience in the publishing industry. Whether you choose a publishing package, marketing package or individual service, you can be assured your manuscript will be handled with care and professionalism. Prices start from $629.

3.) Xlibris Publishing

http://www.xlibris.com

Whether you are writing a book, promoting your work, or searching for online publishing services or a self publisher to publish your book, Xlibris' comprehensive range of publishing, editorial, add-on and marketing services enable you to customize your self-publishing experience. Prices start from $649.

4.) Grosvenor House Publishing

http://www.grosvenorhousepublishing.co.uk

Grosvenor House Publishing Ltd. have worked very hard to offer you, the author, a comprehensive, affordable and quality alternative to the all too often frustrating world of conventional publishing. Prices start from £795.

5.) iUniverse

http://www.iuniverse.com

iUniverse has helped more than 30,000 authors publish their books professionally and affordably. Since 1999, we have crafted a reputation for breaking records and blazing new trails in the self-publishing industry. Prices start from $599.

6.) Outskirts Press

http://www.outskirtspress.com

Outskirts Press offers you the best of both worlds by combining the advantages of independent self-publishing with the advantages of traditional book publishing. Before, during, and after publication you will receive the assistance of a dedicated group of publishing professionals, all the while maintaining 100% of your publishing rights and 100% of your profits. The very Basic package starts at $199.

7.) Love of Books

http://www.loveofbooks.com.au

Love of Books self-publishing- Our job and promise: Is to help individual authors self publish, print and market their new self published book the best way possible. Self-publishing truly is affordable. We offer a large support system... Prices start from around 799AUD.

8.) Author House

http://www.authorhouse.co.uk

AuthorHouse UK can help you place your book in some of the top UK book shops. You will need to fill out some basic information for a quote.

9.) Book Guild Publishing

http://www.bookguildpublishing.com

As an independent publisher, Book Guild Publishing has been providing authors with publishing expertise for 25 years. Under both our mainstream and Partnership Publishing programmes, we offer a full editorial, production, publicity, marketing, sales and distribution service, with the benefit of a high level of creative control and involvement for our authors. You'll need to contact them for a quote, but prices usually start around £599.

10.) Raider Publishing

http://www.raiderpublishing.com

Raider Publishing is the first publisher to offer authors more than fifty percent of their book's royalties, while at the same time, promising to pursue promotional opportunities for you (if desired) after the publishing and distribution is complete. Raider Publishing is revolutionizing the industry. Please explore our site and see for yourself what we can do for you and your work! Prices start from $899.

Top 10 eBook Distributors

1.) Amazon

https://kdp.amazon.com

This is by far the biggest e-Publisher on the web today with over 50% of the market share. It's easy to sign up and get a book on the KDP (Kindle Direct Publishing) platform. With 70% royalties given to all books over $2.99, you can't go wrong. You'll have to do some aggressive promoting at first, but if you make it to the best-sellers list, then Amazon actively markets the book for you.

2.) Smashwords

http://www.smashwords.com

Apart from Amazon, the number one distributor I would use is Smashwords. The reason being is Smashwords offer a service where you submit your book to them, and they in turn, will submit your book to numerous digital distributors on your behalf. Distributors like: Barnes and Nobel, Apple iBookstore, Sony, Kobo, Baker and Taylor, Flipkart, Aldiko and the Diesel ebookstore. For a small 10% commission of the retail price, they will take all the hard work out of publishing online and do it for you. This is a great resource that I highly recommend, however, you will have to do your own marketing, but Smashwords have that covered and offer you a free e-book.

3.) Author Solutions

http://www.authorsolutions.com

Author Solutions are very similar to Smashwords when it comes to digital publishing. You upload your book and cover to them, and they in turn, will deliver it to all the big digital distributors. They provide sales, fulfilment, and customer support. In addition, they also offer web design and a lead generation plan.

4.) Apple

http://www.apple.com/uk/ibooks-author/

If you have a Mac, iPad or even an iPhone, then you can publish your book through iBooks Author. All you need to do is download the app from the app store and your good to go. You need a little bit of technical skill to pull it off, but once you've mastered the process, you can create visually stunning eBooks for all of the Apple devices. Alternatively, you can get Smashwords to do it for you.

5.) Barnes and Nobel

http://www.barnesandnoble.com

This is the third biggest digital publisher on the web. As Amazon has the Kindle, B&N have the Nook. If you decide not to use Smashwords, you have to become a vendor of record before publishing with Barnes and Nobel. Here you'll be able to publish your book for the Nook e-reading device. This page will tell you everything you need to get started: http://www.barnesandnoble.com/help/cds2.asp?PID=8148

6.) Sony

ebookstore.sony.com/publishers/

Sony uses the publisher portal for any author wanting to publish on their Reader store. To start, you'll have to click on the Publisher Info Form and fill in all the details. They will then go over your details and a member of their Content Acquisition Team will get in contact with you. After that, they will discuss what you need to do to get your book into their store.

7.) Kobo

http://www.kobo.com

I don't know much about Kobo only that they use FTP (File Transfer Protocol) to upload your book and they belong to Rakuten Company (the same company that owns Play.com). You will need to sign up for a Kobo Writing Life (KWL) account. They do have guidelines which can be found here: http://www.kobo.com/publishers?style=onestore&language=en-US&language=en-US&store=CA&store=GB

8.) Baker & Taylor.

http://www.baker-taylor.com

As with Kobo, I haven't had any dealings with Baker and Taylor. They have their own bookstores called Axis 360 and the TS 360 so it stands to reason they have quite good digital publishing distribution. I've had a look on the website to try and find out exactly how a self-publisher can publish with them, but I can't really find any literature. It is worthwhile to spend a few minutes browsing their site to see what they have to offer. My advice though is, use Smashwords to get published with Baker and Taylor.

9.) Diesel eBook Store

http://www.diesel-ebooks.com

I bet you didn't know diesel had a bookstore? Well they do, and it's thriving. The good thing about Diesels eBook store is that it is compatible with most popular eReaders like the Kindle, iPad, Nook and Kobo devices. Again, I've had a look on their website and it seems that you need to contact them and inquire how to get your book published in their store. Best bet? Yup, you guessed it, use Smashwords.

10.) Flipkart

http://www.flipkart.com

The only way I can explain Flipkart is like Amazon, but for India. It's an online megastore just for India. Now before you say, why should I publish with these, think about this. India's market for eReaders has exploded in 2013. The population is 1.27 Billion people. So to ignore this market will be foolish. They, much like Amazon have a section of the store completely dedicated to eBooks. Again, it seems that they have made it extremely hard to find out how to publish with them. My advice, if you don't want to use Smashwords, contact their support and ask them how to do it.